THE HANDBOOK FOR BUILDING AND UNLEASHING YOUR PERSONAL BRAND IN THE DIGITAL AGE

MARK W. SCHAEFER
BEST-SELLING AUTHOR OF *THE CONTENT CODE*

This publication is designed to provide accurate and authoritative information in regard to the subject matter covered. It is sold with the understanding that neither the author nor the publisher is engaged in rendering legal, accounting, or other professional service. If legal advice or other expert assistance is required, the services of a competent professional person should be sought. - From a Declaration of Principles jointly adopted by a Committee of the American Bar Association and a Committee of Publishers.

Schaefer Marketing Solutions
www.businessesGROW.com
First Edition: February 2017

Publisher is not responsible for websites (or their content) that are not owned by the publisher.

Cover, Interior Layout and Design by Sarah Mason www.uncommonlysocial.com

Library of Congress Cataloging-in-Publication Data
Schaefer, Mark W.
KNOWN: The Handbook For Building And Unleashing Your Personal Brand
Mark W. Schaefer - 1st ed.
ISBN-10: 0692816062
ISBN: 978-0692816066

I want to dedicate this book to the hundreds of people I've met who worked so hard to become known, the thousands of people out there who will now be on the path to be known, and the one woman who made this possible, Rebecca.

Other Books by Mark W. Schaefer

The Tao of Twitter

Return On Influence

Born to Blog (with Stanford Smith)

Social Media Explained

The Content Code

Contents

The Equity of Influence

*"There is no passion to be found playing small – in settling for a life
that is less than the one you are capable of living."*
–Nelson Mandela

I used to be a big shot.

Before my days as a scrambling entrepreneur, I was a jet-setting executive and among the top 1 percent on the company organizational chart. I'm not telling you this to brag. I'm setting the stage for the drama that came next!

In my corporate career with this Fortune 100 titan, I had been awarded seven patents and two master's degrees.

I managed a highly-visible global team of all-stars.

I had earned two Chairman's Awards for outstanding achievement, a stock award that was the highest recognition in my company. As far as I know, I was the only employee who had earned this award twice.

In my position as Global Director of eBusiness, I was the company's go-to guy for anything internet.

My business life was a frenzy of activity. I received hundreds of emails each day, conference calls from every corner of the world, and a jet stream of opportunity and recognition.

But I was also dabbling in some entrepreneurial side businesses, and once I was assured that my children's college tuition was paid for, I decided it was time to reinvent myself and venture out on my own as a consultant, writer, and college educator.

I'll never forget the eerie thing that happened the morning of my first day on my own. The frenzy was over. No emails. No calls. No meetings in Paris. No communication of any kind. I was facing the Veil of Silence!

In my company, I was well-known and respected. But now that I was starting over, nobody knew me. Nobody in this world knew or cared that I had been a big deal just 24 hours ago.

On my first day as an entrepreneur, I was the go-to guy for nothing.

My friend Cesar Paz, a leading digital innovator and entrepreneur in Brazil, has a similar story. "I used to work for a huge company, Embraer," he told me. "When I left to start out on my own, it was as if I had lost my last name. I used to be Cesar from Embraer. Now nobody knew who I was, or cared. I had to build my brand all over again!"

Like Cesar, in one day it seemed like my hard-built reputation had been swept away. Talk about a humbling experience!

I was back at the starting line. For my brand-new consulting business, my first two customers were a college kid trying to start a catering business and a local real estate agent. My first professional speaking engagement was in front of the Lions Club in Farragut, Tennessee. (The fried chicken served at lunch was delicious, by the way.)

But in less than five years, I built up my own brand reputation that unlocked consulting assignments with some of the biggest companies in the world, including Cisco, Johnson & Johnson, and Adidas. I was in a position to give speeches at convention halls filled with thousands of people. I lectured at some of the world's top universities, and I was a guest speaker at a European "think tank" that had featured some of the most famous authors and diplomats in the world, like Nelson Mandela.

My path to new power was chock-full of mistakes and bad habits that I carried over from the old corporate world. And this is what I learned the hard way: There's a new paradigm of power ... or what I call the new "equity of influence."

What do I mean? In a traditional office job, these are some of the symbols of personal power and influence:

- Job title

- Salary

- Achievements

- Number of direct reports

- Framed degrees and citations on the office wall

- Control of scarce resources

- Where you went to college

- Executive relationships

Studies have even shown that how tall you are, how good-looking you are, and how you dress can contribute to the personal power you achieve in the so-called real world!

But on the internet, *none of this matters.* Nobody knows or cares what your title is. Nobody can really tell how tall you are, how rich you are, or what family you married into. It just doesn't matter.

In fact, there's only one thing that counts today, only one source of power and influence when it comes to the online world. And it is this.

To be known.

And that's what this book is about. I want you to have a more powerful, impactful, and rewarding life by helping you to become known.

Perhaps the idea of being regarded as a leader in your field seems daunting, maybe even unachievable. It's not. I'll tell you stories of very common people from all over the world who have become uncommonly successful. All of them started at ground zero and followed precisely the same four steps to become known, everywhere, every time. I'll provide a detailed, step-by-step guide to show how you can follow these steps, too.

What's in it for you?

I'm going to stop talking about me. Let's discuss how this new way of thinking relates to you and your personal goals.

Where do you want to go with your career and your life? What's next?

Here are some of the dreams and goals I've heard from my friends and clients. They want to ...

- Write a book

- Launch a speaking career

- Become a consultant

- Be named to a prestigious board

- Remain relevant in their field for many years

- Help attract donations for a charity

- Sell digital products online

- Run for political office

- Achieve recognition for their work

- Earn a university teaching position

- Become a paid "influencer"

- Be in a better position for a promotion

- Share their passion and ideas to make the world a better place

In the process of helping my friends find a path to achieve these dreams, I heard myself delivering the same advice over and over: "Well … to achieve that goal, you have to become known."

I began to realize that there are so many personal and professional goals today that simply can't be achieved without being known!

Maybe you're like my friend Alisa Meredith, an independent marketing professional. When she heard I was writing this book, she sent me a note: "I want to be known. It's not about being famous. I'd rather just make a good living quietly. But I'm a horrible salesperson. My hope is that if people come to know me, it will be easier for me to connect with the new customers I want to work with."

Certainly, it would work that way for Alisa.

This is the kind of thinking IBM uses when it encourages its many scientists and engineers to blog and create videos. Many of them have attracted passionate fans through their insightful content, so when they walk into a sales meeting for the first time, there's instant credibility in the room. They've essentially pre-populated the sales relationship!

Being known is not the same as being famous. It's not about having millions of fans and red carpet appearances. Being known is about having the proper authority, reputation, and audience to realize your potential and achieve your goals ... whatever they might be.

Passion without a plan is a hobby

The "personal branding" space is pretty crowded. Amazon has more than 3,000 books on the subject. It seems that everybody has advice on how to be famous, become a guru, or establish yourself as an "influencer."

What makes this book any different?

Most of the self-help available on the subject of personal branding starts and stops with "discover your passion." But then what?

We live in a world filled with intoxicating mythology, like "If you can dream it, you can be it." I don't know about you, but I'm not going to hang my future on a dream. I need a plan. And I think you probably need one, too.

Finding your passions and strengths is important, but that's the starting line, not the finish line. You need to be known for SOMETHING in a relevant space large enough for it to MATTER. You need to create content in a way that makes a difference and builds an audience you can ACTIVATE.

While the prevailing guru-speak may urge you to ignore the rest of the world and simply follow your dream, I'd like to offer different advice. Let's think this through. It may take years of work to become known. Why not be smart about it, plot out a real strategy, and give yourself the very best chance to succeed? Would you rather blindly follow a dream with almost no chance of success, or save yourself those years of wasted effort by logically determining a path that gives you a higher probability of accomplishing your goals?

Dana Hitt Sanchez provides coaching to small business owners and has seen too many crash and burn when they run on passion without a plan. "A passion and a hobby is about you," she said. "It's an activity that gives YOU pleasure and may be removed from reality. The scary thing is, I see so many people devoting their lives to a dream because it's their passion and they just think if they 'build it, people will come.' I mean, if I love it, won't everyone else? Maybe. But probably not if you don't have a plan. Just concentrating on a hobby doesn't answer a need."

Think of your personal brand as a start-up, the start-up of YOU. Research shows that more than 95 percent of start-ups fail, and the number one reason for failure – by far – is that there was no market need for the product. By following the logical path in this book, you'll have the very best shot to combine an idea that you love with an audience that will help you succeed.

I'm going to tip the balance in your favor by helping you work through

- The true role of "passion" in your new personal brand.

- The fact that you do NOT have to be an expert in anything to start your journey.

- Strategies to find your distinct niche and voice.

- Nine ways to stand out, even in a very crowded marketplace.

- The importance of creating content to help fulfill your dream. But that's not just any content – it's the content that is precisely right for you.Plans to identify and build an audience that will help you activate your goals.

- Measuring success and knowing if it's time to quit or pivot.

Known is the first book of its kind to teach you, step by step, how the most successful people online focus their efforts, create a plan, and activate their personal brand in a measurable way. This is the practical handbook for achieving extraordinary personal power in the digital age.

But we're not here by ourselves. I brought along some fascinating friends. This book features incredible case studies starring people who started with almost nothing and became known in a way that helped them succeed in art, real estate, construction, publishing, education, sports, medicine, finance, fashion, and many other fields. And they all followed a similar path, a path to become known, a path available to anybody today.

You'll see through these stories that it doesn't matter what you look like, the color of your skin, where you live, how old you are, or how much money you have. It makes no difference where you've been before, how dark and difficult your life has been, or how many injustices you've endured. Today, everyone has a chance to transform, to become something bold and wonderful and new, to have a meaningful voice in the world.

I am living proof of this.

I started this chapter talking about my personal transition from the corporate world to forming my own business. Around the time I embarked on my own journey to be known, I was also suffering through the darkest period of my life.

My wife, an addict who I had supported through many cycles of rehab and recovery, ran away with another man. She took with her my two young stepchildren whom I had raised and loved as my own. I never saw them again. Stepparents have no rights. We went through a brutal divorce, and I was forced to give her half of my net worth. Since she had never worked, I had to pay off her bills from addiction recovery centers, even after we were divorced.

And I had medical bills of my own. I had suffered a spinal cord injury and had been briefly paralyzed on the left side of my body. Doctors wondered if I would have long-term problems walking. After months of therapy and a surgery to place a metal plate in my head, I was on a road to physical recovery.

In this same time period, I lost three of my best friends – two to disease and one from a self-inflicted gunshot wound.

Losing my family, my health, my friends, and my financial well-being was nearly too much to bear. I suffered from depression and could barely function at times. When I started my process to become known in the digital world, I was at emotional ground zero. Perhaps below zero, if that's possible.

But I clawed my way back. I found my "voice," my place in the world. I found an audience that mattered. I worked hard to connect to people with relevant and entertaining content like blog posts and podcasts. I was consistent and patient for years.

Today I'm known as an expert in digital marketing, but I didn't start that way. When I published my first blog post, I knew nothing about blogging. When I started consulting, I knew very little about consulting. When I wrote my first book, I had never done anything like that before.

As you'll learn, becoming known is an *evolutionary process*. You don't have to be an expert in something to ultimately succeed as long as you embrace a mindset of continuous and urgent learning.

This book will inspire you, nurture you, and challenge you to reach higher. It will change your perspective on what it takes to win in business today, and it may even change your life.

Now, it's time to begin with the first question you should always ask before embarking on something so exciting and new: "Why?"

CHAPTER 1

Can Anybody Become Known?

"I want to put a ding in the universe." – Steve Jobs

In my research, I found a staggering amount of information on becoming web-famous. In fact, Google returned 84 million results, but here's my favorite entry:

The Idiot's Guide to Becoming Famous with Minimal Effort [1]

Step 1. Do something incredibly stupid and obnoxious to attract attention to yourself.

Step 2. Be sure to record your act of stupidity and publish it on YouTube.

Step 3. Get rewarded for your idiocy and bask in your new-found fame. Just make sure they spell your name correctly.

There are lots of ways to become both famous and infamous on the web, but that's not the same as becoming "known."

In this chapter, I'm shining a light on the important questions. Why do you need to be known at all? Can anybody become known? Is there a niche for everybody? Do you (yes, YOU!) have what it takes to be known?

And at the end of this chapter, I'll launch the step-by-step process we'll follow together for the rest of the book.

First, let's address some of the tough questions that might be on your mind.

Why do you need to be known at all?

When I was starting out in life, the channels for building influence were much different – and much more dysfunctional – than they are today. To be known in the world back then, you needed to go to the right university, get a job with a proper company or investment bank, cozy up to the right establishment people, and perhaps marry into a family of influence so you had a powerful name and money behind you. When I applied for my first professional job, I was turned down because the company only hired people from Ivy League schools. (I fought my way into the company any way!)

Before the Internet Age, you had less control of your own destiny. The world of my youth wasn't digital, it wasn't global, it wasn't connected. So to succeed, you spent your time jumping through hurdles. You played the politics. You sucked-up to a boss. You "paid your dues." That seemed to be the only way to get ahead and get noticed.

Those days are over my friend, or at least they can be if you take advantage of the opportunity before you.

We live in an amazing time. The power has shifted – to YOU! If you have access to a connected device and the internet, you have the opportunity to be known for something, to connect with people who need you, who want to learn from you, who want to be like you.

Anyone can publish content and create their own power and influence in this world. The examples I use in this book are from common people – bankers, construction workers, real estate agents, teachers, and others who struggled in so many ways before they were known. Many suffered and perhaps were even on the brink of personal disaster. But by becoming known, they transformed their lives into something original, brave, and, in many cases, highly profitable.

One of my favorite case studies from my book *Return On Influence* is the story of a timid young man who dropped out of school to become a clerk in a camera store. He began blogging and creating videos about his favorite technologies, and soon his influential content was affecting the fortunes of Silicon Valley titans. Tens of thousands of industry insiders trusted his views as he transformed himself from camera nerd into one of the most powerful tech bloggers in the world – the true story of Robert Scoble.

It's come down to this: Magazines and television networks feel like detached institutions, while influencers are real people, relatable individuals, our virtual friends. We identify with our favorite online personalities, and we become loyal followers. The authenticity of those who become known on the web today converts to trust and we take their advice.

Stepping out

Traditional editors, television anchors, and Wall Street execs once got the perks and exclusive access. Now the extravagant stays at beach mansions and the first-class flights go to influencers. The paydays are becoming staggering. Snapchat star Logan Paul earned $200,000 for one day of filming on a Dunkin' Donuts commercial. He's only 21.

Maybe you don't care about fame and fortune. Perhaps it's simply the time to become known because it's your turn to let your light shine.

My friend Larry C. Lewis spent more than a decade working

behind the scenes in the high-profile jewelry industry before deciding it was time to come out from the shadows. "I worked in marketing for well-known companies in the fashion and jewelry industry," he said. "On the side, I was a master seller on eBay, ran campaigns for national artists, a movie theater, a college, and the Waldorf Astoria hotel at one point. But I always worked behind the scenes in the name of others.

"About a year ago, I started feeling depressed. I have dreams of my own, yet I was living someone else's dream. I had projects in my heart that were getting buried, and as time passed my ideas became obsolete. No matter how much I was getting paid or how successful I made someone else, I was still living in their shadow. I felt limited. I knew I had to step out on my own and become known if I wanted to reach my full potential.

"Stepping out – that's a hard decision to make," Lewis said. "I'm very comfortable working in the background promoting other people, and I don't like being in the spotlight myself. But I realized that if I wanted to keep a roof over my head and remain relevant, I have to avoid being comfortable. Unless of course I want to keep sponsoring other dreams and not my own."

In this tumultuous world, there are only two transferrable assets we have: our education and being "known." What's the probability there will be a change in your employment status in the next five years? If you're a relative unknown in your industry, you'll have to compete for a new job like everybody else. But if you're known, you'll have an instant advantage, a permanent advantage, perhaps the only advantage you need to overcome that adversity.

Do you feel determined to reach for something more like Larry? I hope you do. We live in an utterly amazing age where everybody has a shot at being known. It's time to Take. Your. Shot.

Like Antonio Centeno.

Can anybody become known?

Antonio Centeno[2] was a proud member the U.S. Marine Corps for five years, returned home after the Iraq War, and realized he had no marketable skills … he couldn't even type. Today, he runs some of the most widely recognized men's fashion sites on the web. He's a sought-after speaker, a YouTube star, author, and the founder of his own national style conference.

Here's how he made this remarkable transition, in his own words:

I grew up in a dusty trailer park in West Texas and didn't have much as a kid. I joined the Marines when I was a young man and became an officer. When I first put on the Marines uniform, I felt different. It changed the way I thought about myself. I had never experienced this feeling before. A Marine always looks sharp. It was amazing how my appearance changed my attitude and my confidence.

After I got out of the service, I wanted to get married to my girlfriend. When I was shopping for a suit to wear for my wedding, I tried on a $3,000 custom suit. Of course I couldn't afford it, but I was like "Wow, this thing is amazing!" I saw the power of how a suit can make you feel. It was that same feeling of self-esteem and respect I had whenever I wore that Marines uniform.

Through these experiences, I began to make connections that made me realize appearance matters a lot. But I didn't do anything with that observation at first. At that point in my life, I needed a job. So, I went to business school at the University of Texas, and right out of college I was hired to work in finance at a manufacturing plant in Wisconsin. It wasn't for me. I didn't fit. Within three months, I was fired.

Being out of work gave me a chance to assess what I loved to do in life and I couldn't get this idea out of my head about how your appearance affects your attitude and success. I felt so strongly that how you dress can have a positive effect on your life. But when I looked around the country, it seemed like a lot of Americans didn't believe that. So I saw this amazing opportunity and I created my first company: A Tailored Suit.

For four years, I struggled with an online business that made custom clothing. I learned that I didn't have a good business plan to sell suits, but I also learned that I could create content about men's fashion very, very well. People weren't buying my suits, but thousands of people were reading my blog posts!

Each day I'd get up at about four in the morning and write these amazing articles. Actually, I dictated them. I never did learn to type! My articles about clothing tips attracted a large audience. To this day, those first articles still get about a 100,000 visitors a month. I realized that I was pretty good at creating content about fashion and success. So I started writing fashion content for other web sites. I was becoming known through this content and I thought I could actually turn it into a business. So I started the "Real Men Real Style" information portal.

There's a lot of fashion advice out there, but what makes me unique is I always deliver something of value and I'm always authentic. Also, I saw that a lot of the content in the fashion field was being written, and that the video format was wide open. That's how I separated myself from the pack, by creating short fashion tip videos.

I took some chances and went from a guy with literally no job skills to somebody who is known in the fashion business. I'm providing well for my family, and I'm doing work that I love.

My success didn't come from just having a "passion." I solved a burning problem that people with money are willing to pay for. You need that great idea, the content, and the audience willing to pay, and then BOOM, you're in business. I'm surprised how many people can't figure that out.

If I had to name my passion, it might be motorcycles. But I didn't want to become an expert in motorcycles. I wanted to find an interest that I could leverage for the long term. My goal is to build and sustain a business that's successful enough that I can give my children the option to do whatever they want in their lives … something I never had.

I love Antonio's story, and his message is a theme you'll see in every case study in this book: The key to success isn't necessarily a passion, it's finding a *sustainable interest*, and I'll help you find yours in the next chapter.

Another key component of becoming known is producing consistent content. When he discovered a promising, un-saturated niche for himself – video-based fashion tips – Antonio committed to creating 200 style videos in 200 days – for less than $2,000 (including his equipment).

"Yes, it can be nerve-wracking to put yourself out there," he said. "And yes, my first videos were terrible. But the more content you create, the better you become, and it gets easier, and even fun. If you commit, great things happen. Why did I do 200 videos in a row? Because it forced me to learn.

"A lot of people think this level of content production is unattainable. They think they're not a writer, they're not a video person. Well, guess what? I'm not a writer. I'm not a video person. I started at the bottom with literally no skills."

Two of the powerful lessons I learned from writing this book are that years of hard work are often mistaken for innate talent and that perseverance is more indispensable to your success than genius. You might assume that being known for something is an unattainable goal because you're not the best at something. The people you'll meet in this book share a trait with Antonio: They didn't start as natural experts in anything. They became known through commitment, constancy, and repeated practice.

To be known, you don't have to be a subject matter expert. But you must have the determination and patience to become one. A professional is simply an amateur who didn't quit.

Antonio, like the other stars of *KNOWN*, continues to push himself and learn. After he created his 200 videos in 200 days, he told me his next goal was to tackle 1,000 videos in 1,000 days. "Think how good I will be by then!" he told me.

"I'm not a huge YouTube star," Antonio said. "None of my videos have gone viral. I'm slowly building my audience. I'm not trying to hit home runs. But you can still win a baseball game with lots of singles and doubles. Even if a few people are watching, these are the people who come to know me, trust me, and eventually buy something."

Today, Antonio makes enough money that he can easily afford that $3,000 suit he tried on all those years ago – or any suit, for that matter. He has monetized his content through web advertising, books, coaching, webinars, and his own style conference.

I included this story because if Antonio Centeno can rise

from the West Texas trailer park with literally no marketable skills, perhaps you'll see that you can overcome your obstacles and become known, too.

There are elements of Antonio's story that illustrate the foundational processes we'll explore together in this book:

- Finding the right *place.* For Antonio, fashion advice was a sustainable interest.

- Finding the right *space.* Fashion tip videos were a wide-open niche in his market.

- Producing *consistent content.* He created 200 videos in 200 days, and then another 1,000 after that! The ex-Marine wasn't a fashion expert. He learned his way to success.

- Building a *meaningful audience.* Over time, he built one that was big enough to monetize and matter.

- Exercising *patience.* He worked hard for four years before seeing a significant payoff. He's building his business slowly instead of hoping for a viral success. He kept moving forward as long as he was making progress.

Let's look at two more unusual success stories – from the very different worlds of fitness and art – to get a feel for the process of becoming known in the digital age. As you read these amazing stories, look for some common lessons:

1. What made them stand out in a crowded niche?

2. What was the role of publishing content in their success?

3. How did they acquire their audience?

4. How long did it take for them to "make it"?

Case study: Putting some muscle into it[3]

Just a few years ago, Joe Wicks was a down-on-his-luck personal trainer who spent his days cycling around London, pasting up posters in city train stations for his sparsely attended fitness classes. Now the "Body Coach," as he calls himself, is known throughout the United Kingdom, primarily through his million-strong following on social media.

Once the 31-year-old trainer discovered Instagram as a channel for establishing his brand, his feed became a conveyor belt of 15-second recipe videos, before-and-after client photos, and pictures of himself flexing his muscles. "I Snapchat in the bath," Joe said in a press interview. "I Snapchat when I wake up. I'm giving people inspiration. It's like a TV show."

Joe's popularity today is staggering but not all that surprising. He's found his PLACE: a handsome, charismatic man with an incredibly simple 90-day fitness and nutrition plan. But his SPACE is what really made him a star. There are plenty of good-looking fitness experts in the world, but none of them were tapping into the needs of the under-30 crowd on Instagram and Snapchat. His key to success wasn't just "passion." He always loved fitness. His fortunes only tipped when he found a meaningful social media audience that could help him succeed.

Once he found his audience, Joe's star continued to rise. His first cookbook, *Lean In 15,* was a nonfiction bestseller. Every day, around 400 people sign up for his 90-day body transformation plan (paying about $200 for the privilege). With a new book deal, a TV show, and lucrative product endorsements, he's now earning $1 million a month.

It's not fame that motivates him. He's driven by a higher purpose: "I want to be the voice that gets the nation healthy."

It's a message that's a bit controversial. He's bothered by what he considers the fallacy of low-calorie diets and ruthlessly calls out the weight-loss industry's major players for encouraging a fear of fat and promoting punishing programs that ultimately fail because they're unsustainable.

"We've been taught that calories are evil," he said.[4] "Most diets are based on 'we weigh you every week, you come back, buy our low-fat chocolate bars, you keep coming back.' That's why you've got women in diet clubs for 20 years. How insane is that?"

Joe Wicks struggled for years on the brink of financial ruin before he was able to combine a sustainable interest, meaningful content, and a distribution channel that connected with an audience who loves him. Nothing worked until he became known.

Case study: Paintings for ants

Since the beginning of time, it's been tough for artists to become known. There's truth behind the characterization of a "starving artist." One study showed that just 20 percent of all artists can make a living from their craft. Artists earn about half the sale price for works sold in a gallery and usually nothing from resale in the private auction houses, where the sky-high prices reward early collectors, not the creators.

Lorraine Loots beat those odds by finding both a *place* and a *space* that allowed her to become known and successful on her own terms.

Lorraine, who is from South Africa, has always loved art, but she initially followed a more "sensible" career path, spending several years working in social media marketing. She hated it. So she started freelancing as a marketer, and while holding down 12 different jobs at one time, she enrolled in a class on "Business for Artists."

The final class project was to create a business plan for her art projects. And "365 Paintings for Ants" was born.

"The plan was that I would set aside an hour a day outside of my 'real job' to complete an artwork," she said. "So ironically, the idea came about after I had decided that I didn't want to pursue a career as an artist at all.

"I committed to spending one hour a day creating something. The only thing I could finish in that timeframe was a miniature, and so I was sort of forced into a niche!"

And so, every day since January 1, 2013, Lorraine Loots has created an intricate painting that is 10-by-10 centimeters, not much bigger than a large coin. Her subjects range from stunning scenery to celebrities, animals to iconic book covers. Some of the tiny paintings now take as long as nine hours to complete.

Lorraine started posting her tiny daily masterpieces on Instagram. After receiving an outpouring of support from fans, she committed to another 365 days of constant painting ... and has never stopped. Today, her paintings sell instantly, and her work has been displayed in some of the most famous galleries in the world.

While her success is certainly attributed to her remarkable talent, her ability to stand out in the desperately competitive world of art was due to her unique *place* – daily miniature paintings – and her *space* for publishing – Instagram.

"As the popularity of my project spread," she said, "interest grew to see exactly what I would paint every day. People would follow along on Instagram to see what I painted, and whether I'd be able to complete the challenge every day!

"I was also lucky to have quite a few influential blogs pick up on the project, and I was featured on Colossal (an important art and design site), which was a huge turning point. After that, Instagram featured me on their home page, and then it all just snowballed."

Consistency of content – a painting every day – has been part of Lorraine's claim to fame, and it's a pace that's not easy to maintain. "I've been so sick that sometimes I was only able to drag myself out of the bed for that hour it takes to do the painting, and it's taken all my willpower. We lost a close family member at the end of 2013. That was incredibly hard. Life just goes on and sometimes you have to make big sacrifices if you want to stay committed.

"Finding my niche and becoming known has been rewarding on so many levels. On a financial level of course, it's every artist's dream to be able to make a living producing the work they want to. Knowing that I can help support my family doing this strange thing means I wake up with a surreal sense of contentedness every day.

"On an achievement level, finishing the first two years of consecutive daily paintings was the hardest thing I'd ever done, and I'll always be proud of myself for sticking it out no matter what happened (and of course, a lot happened!). I also feel like I have the ability to make a real difference in the world. By being known, I can contribute to causes I support through auctions of my art, and I can promote other artists, places, and products that I believe in.

"Initially, I thought of the project as a massive challenge, like a marathon I would be relieved to have survived. And it really was. But it also became this meditative time; a quiet and almost sacred part of each day. And as the days went by and the end of the 365 days came closer, I got sadder and sadder thinking that I'd have to stop. Then I realized that this project was mine, and if I wanted to keep doing it, I could. And so I did."

An unlikely success? Blind luck?

No, there's something more. We're beginning to see a pattern emerge, a common route to success, an achievable path found in each story and interview.

The common path

As you read the case studies in this book, note how every person started out as an unknown and used content to unleash a powerful digital presence that propelled their dreams.

In the case of Antonio Centeno, he admittedly had neither job prospects nor marketable skills before he found success through his blog and unique short-form fashion videos.

Trainer Joe Wicks was flat-broke before he honed his controversial fitness message and found an audience on social media who loved it.

Lorraine Loots didn't necessarily find her niche through any magnificent plan. She stumbled on it through a commitment to paint something every day for a year. But it resulted in her distinctive place, miniature art, that allowed her to become known and empowered her to support favorite charities and fellow artists. In fact, each of these people mentioned that a purpose beyond money helps keep them going.

But can ANYBODY do it?

I'll put it this way. *Everybody has the chance to be known* and realize their goals and dreams, but not everybody will succeed. Some will listen to the gurus and "follow their dream" into oblivion without the plan they need to give them a chance to succeed. Some will grow impatient and give up too soon. Many will be unwilling to devote the time and consistent hard work needed to make it happen.

So, no. Not everybody will become known for something in this world, but I believe completely and with all of my heart that **every person has the potential to do it,** if they faithfully follow the path in this book ... and maybe get some help where needed. Let me explain what I mean.

I once had a student who took the same university marketing class from me three semesters in a row. I felt kind of bad that she was hearing the same stories and lessons for the third time, but she was desperate to learn how to be effective on the web and get her eco-friendly craft business online.

As I got to know her, I realized that she was very bright, had a great idea for a business, and was an excellent storyteller. But she may have been the most disorganized person I've ever known. She was never going to succeed in any business venture, let alone becoming known online, unless she worked on her organizational skills. She knew that she needed to learn from me, but she was incapable of following though and executing.

Can she become known? Yes. But she'll need somebody to help her stay focused!

Getting help

The lesson here is that everybody's different ... the glory of human diversity! You may find that there's a part of this book that feels like a barricade, but that doesn't mean you can't succeed. If you don't have the time, talent, and skills to make it completely on your own, there are lots of resources available to help you, and we'll cover them throughout this book. If you find there are gaps in your ability to be known, remember there are work-arounds.

Over the past two years I've done a deep dive on this fascinating idea of becoming known, and I've never found a successful person who said "Either you have it or you don't." Everything you need to succeed can come through focus, patience, practice, determination ... and maybe an editor or virtual assistant to keep you organized!

What if I'm shy and don't like promoting myself?

On a speaking assignment in The Netherlands a few years ago, I ended my talk with what I thought was an inspirational call to action: "Today, we all have the capacity to publish online and find our voice and power in the world," I said. "All of us can become known and turn our knowledge into influence on the web."

More or less the subject of this book, right?

Afterward, a number of people in the largely Dutch audience came up to me to politely compliment me on my speech … and correct me. They said that in their culture, people would never try to stand out on the web. In fact, they're rewarded for fitting in, not becoming known. They had a local saying that "if you try to stand out we will bop you on the nose." I might not have that exactly right, but the sentiment is close!

In other parts of the world, this is known as the tall poppy syndrome – people of high status are resented and criticized because they're classified as better than their peers.

What I learned is that "being known" isn't necessarily a challenge for people who are shy. It may be a problem for an entire nation of people because of their culture.

Now, here's the second discussion that occurred after the same talk in The Netherlands. A group of people near me commented on the bold and entertaining speaking style of the American keynote speakers. "Why don't we have speakers like this in our own country?" they asked. "Why don't we have thought leaders from Holland taking the stage at our conferences?"

The reason is simple. They're not known.

Today, you're not just contending with others who are known in your city, region, or country. You're competing with people who are known throughout the world. As economist Thomas Friedman famously wrote, the world is flat.

I understand the cultural constraints that might be holding you in place, and perhaps you're satisfied living in a world where you get "bopped on the nose" for standing out. But you must also realize that you have almost no hope of competing in a global marketplace unless you're known. Do you have a choice?

All things being equal, the person who's known has a better chance of getting the job, the teaching position, the customers, or the invitation to speak in The Netherlands.

As I was writing this book, I received a call from a friend who invited me to speak at one of the biggest marketing conferences in the world. We started talking about my life before my blog and my books, the days before I was "known."

He said to me, "We've been friends for five years and I had no idea you had achieved all that stuff in the corporate world. I guess it never came up before."

"Let me ask you something," I said. "None of that matters anyway, does it? I mean, the only reason you're inviting me to this conference is because I'm known, right?"

"I guess that's true," he admitted.

Of course, I already I knew this, but my friend confirmed this core principle. The person who's known gets the business.

Let's turn to the concept of personality type. What if you're shy? Perhaps the idea of putting yourself out there is terrifying because you're timid or afraid of appearing stupid in front of an audience. Maybe you don't think you have anything to add to the conversation in this big world.

Here's a description of a person who might feel uncomfortable becoming known:

- Introverted

- Hates crowds

- Prefers to work alone

- Insecure about publishing content

- Fears the idea of public speaking

The person I'm describing is me, as I embarked on my journey to be known many years ago ... and in some respects, it's still me today. I'm an introvert. I have never pushed the "publish" button on a piece of content without some consternation. I've never taken a stage to give a speech without some fear, and I still hate crowds!

But I've found a system that works for me and my personality, and as you'll discover in the chapters ahead, a person of any temperament can find success and become known.

Is there a niche for everybody?

Here's a secret that's overlooked by most of the personal branding gurus: Becoming known is not about carefully crafting an image or having the most "followers." It's about gaining acceptance.

To become known, your message must be accepted and amplified by people who choose to follow you. No amount of promotion, advertising, or SEO trickery will accomplish that. There's no shortcut.

To be known is a privilege to be earned. Your brand isn't exactly about you. It's about how others *experience* you.

That requires a different mindset, doesn't it?

A principal concept of this book is that image is not enough. Passion is not enough. Becoming known requires finding a sustainable interest (your place) and the right audience that accepts you (your space). We'll be spending the next part of this book exploring those thoughts.

And I'm convinced anybody can do it. Do you think you're

too old to start? Too young? Let me prove you wrong on both counts.

In her excellent book *Grit*, psychologist Angela Duckworth provides original research that shows that older people – even those in their 60s and beyond – are better-equipped than younger people to stick with a project with persistence and consistency.[5]

She writes, "It's possible that adults in their seventh decade of life are grittier because they grew up in a very different cultural era, perhaps one whose values and norms emphasized sustained perseverance more than has been the case recently. In other words, it could be that the Greatest Generation is grittier than the Millennials because cultural forces are different today than yesterday.

"This explanation for why grit and age go hand in hand was suggested to me by an older colleague who, looking over my shoulder at the data, shook his head and said, 'I knew it! I've been teaching undergraduates the same course at the same university for decades. And I'll tell you, they just don't work as hard these days as they used to!'

"My dad, who gave his entire professional life as a chemist to DuPont and quite literally retired with the gold watch, might say the same of the Wharton entrepreneur who approached me after my lecture. Even while pulling all-nighters for his present venture, the young man expected to be on to the next new thing in a few years."

Older people may be better "conditioned" to work consistently and become known than younger people.

Now, what about if you're young and just starting out?

I guest-lecture at many universities, and a common concern among students is that they're still in college and haven't developed any expertise. How can they become known for anything at all? But everyone is original and unique, even if you're just starting out in this world.

One of the young women I've had the honor to mentor is Lindsey Kirchoff. The Tufts University student knew she had to do something bold to attract attention in a very competitive job market, and although she was just 20, she found a niche that created amazing results:

It was a very scary time to think about being a college graduate.

At the university, I minored in Entrepreneurial Leadership Studies and learned about inbound marketing. Instead of interrupting customers with advertising messages, inbound marketing encourages the use of social media and content to get found and build relationships with customers. It seemed to me that this was a good way to look for a job, too. Instead of just sending out resumes and saying "Hey, look at me!" I decided to apply those same principles and create something of value that people would actually want to see.

I needed to show what I could do, not just tell people, so I created a blog called "How to Market to Me." I simply wrote about my observations on marketing and advertising campaigns that I thought hit the mark, or missed the mark, with millennials. Writing these articles gave me a new sense of purpose, and a title: millennial marketing blogger. Even though I wasn't employed, I was working, and publishing on LinkedIn and my blog gave me the platform to show it.

I also made a concerted effort to build a specific audience of people who might hire me. Rather than applying to any job opening, I narrowed my focus to interesting companies I found through blogging and researching my industry. By publishing on LinkedIn I hoped these individuals would start to see some of my work."

And they did. Not only did Kirchoff find employment shortly after graduation, because of her blog, she became known and sought-after.

- She was invited to keynote an automotive conference with a talk about millennial car-buying behaviors.

- She was quoted in *The Los Angeles Times* for insights into millennial habits.

- Campbell's Soup's CEO recruited her to participate in a millennial think tank.

- She collaborated with futurologist Faith Popcorn as member of her Brain Reserve.

- She was featured in self-help author Paul Angone's book *101 Secrets for Your 20s*.

- ... and of course now she's here!

Of all the young job-seeking grads in the country, why did these opportunities come to Lindsey? Because she was known.

Was Lindsey the smartest student in the country? The richest? The hardest-working? As you'll see, intelligence, experience, and even having the best idea are secondary to finding a niche that matters and the tenacity to dominate it.

The age of the people featured in *KNOWN* range from 19 to 65. All of them followed a similar path to success, the path we are entering now.

Are you starting to get excited about the possibilities? Now that I've set the stage, it's time to get into the heart of the book. In the following chapters, we'll step though a linear process to become known:

Step One: Finding your place. You must be known for SOMETHING. What is your unique voice, your distinctive place, your sustainable interest on the web? I'll introduce several extraordinary exercises to help you get there.

Step Two: Finding your space. You must occupy a large enough space to make a difference. I'll help you zoom in on a space that matters.

Step Three: Finding your fuel. Content is the fuel for building a personal brand today. I'll walk you through a process to determine the precise type of content that's best for you, as well as some ideas on producing content that will cut through the clutter.

Step Four: Creating an actionable audience. Your network is your net worth. How do you connect to the critical audience in your space in a way that is actionable and helps you achieve your goals?

We'll also look at taking your brand to the next level, how to determine if your effort is working or not, strategies to sustain your brand for the long-term, and recommendations on what to do if it all isn't working out.

The people we've met so far have all become known by finding their unique place in the world.

Now, it's time to find yours.

Note: There is a workbook available through Amazon to accompany this book called "The KNOWN Personal Branding Workbook." This workbook has bonus content and opportunities to record your responses to the exercises in this book.

CHAPTER 2

Step One: Your Place

"Different is better than better."
– Sally Hogshead, author of "Fascinate"

I've come to detest the phrase "personal branding" because it's been driven into an almost worthless place by so many authors and gurus. Here's where most of the advice falls short: The self-help crowd puts you through a battery of tests to help you find your passion ... and then everything stops ... right ... there.

Gary Vaynerchuk, the frenetically famous sage of wine, business, and hustle, provides this advice to people who want to create a successful personal brand:

"What's the one thing you would want to do for the rest of your life ... you have to pick just one. It's about suffocating all your other options and finding that one thing. Don't worry about the audience, don't worry about the money. When you wake up in the morning, face yourself in the mirror and ask yourself, what do I want to do today and every day most of all? Now go do that. Make that your life's work."[1]

I admire Gary and love the way he has energized so many of his followers to be bold, take risks, and work hard. But we disagree on this point.

I don't think you should blast headlong into any lifelong commitment without at least a bit of forethought. Maybe you should even have a plan.

Time is precious. Why waste years pursuing a passion with a high probability of failure when you can do a little research to give yourself the very best chance to succeed?

Of course it's important to find something you love, your voice, your distinctiveness in this big world. But finding your passion is not nearly enough. How do you *put that passion to work to achieve your goals?*

Breaking through the mantra of passion

I've interviewed nearly 100 individuals about what it takes to be known, and every person has mentioned the same word. Rather than the intensity of passion, what comes up again and again is achieving *consistency* over time. In fact, nearly every person has said that consistency is the most important element in the journey to be known.

Passion ... that's common. Endurance is rare.

We can even look to Gary Vaynerchuk as an example. When he was 22, he probably didn't describe his "look in the mirror" passion as selling wine or building a digital agency, the things he's known for today.

His passion as a young man was (and still is) professional football, specifically the New York Jets. His first business as a teenager was selling collectable football and baseball cards. Perhaps he could have made a career in the sports marketing industry, but Gary has an exceptional business sense and probably knew even back then that this was a long shot. Instead, he focused his "hustle" on something with a better probability of success – growing his father's existing wine business through his compelling and entertaining video presence.

If Gary had followed his youthful passion and started a blog about the Jets or trading cards, perhaps we would have never heard his voice over the din of the thousands of others doing the same thing. He found a space that worked for him – energetic wine videos – and very wisely doubled down! How many wine videos did he make? More than 1,000!

Passion is important, but you also have to consider the commitment, your ability to *sustain* your hustle, and the possibility of having an audience out there who actually cares about what you do. Over the long haul, if you can't connect with an audience big enough to matter, what in the world are you doing?

In his book *So Good They Can't Ignore You*, Georgetown University professor Cal Newport wrote that being passionate about your work is a great goal. However, "following your passion" is not going to get you there because there are two fundamental problems.

The first is that "follow your passion" assumes that people have a pre-existing passion they can identify and use to make career decisions. However, most people have no idea what they want to do and can end up feeling lost.

The second problem lies in the assumption that if you really like something, then you'll really like doing it for a job. "We don't have much evidence that's true," Newport said. "If you study people with meaning and passion in their work, it has little to do with whether the topic of their job matches their pre-existing passions."

He gives an example of amateur photographers or bakers who open businesses but end up facing extreme financial difficulty that leads to unhappiness. "That's because having work that you love is a lot more complicated than, 'Hey, I like this thing! If I do it for work, I'll like my work!'" he explained.

The formula for success isn't simply finding a passion or even a niche. It's finding the magical intersection of *place* and *space* that will give you the best shot at becoming known and successful. I'll jump ahead for a moment to define place and space because this is what I want to do, and you're powerless to stop me.

- **Place:** A sustainable interest and what you want to be known for

- **Space:** An uncontested or under-occupied niche with enough people to matter

In this chapter and the next, we'll work on place, and then I'll help you find your perfect space. Sound like a plan?

Your sustainable interest

A sustainable interest is something that you love, a topic you'll have fun with for years to come. But it's also a theme you want to be known for, something that will help you achieve your long-term life goals.

Let me illustrate the difference between passion and sustainable interest through a personal example.

If I woke up in the morning, looked in the mirror, and asked myself what I want to do more than anything else, it would be to sit on my boat in the middle of a clear blue lake and read a book. I could probably start a blog reporting on the progress of my boat reading. Maybe I could fire up a podcast about what other people are reading on their boats ("Boats & Books!"). I could snap a picture of myself getting sunburned on the boat each day and post it to Instagram. But this isn't a sustainable interest because I would eventually get bored with my boat reading. Sure, it's a passion, but I simply could not sustain that behavior every single day for months and years.

Another passion of mine is hiking. I live in one of the most beautiful places in America, Tennessee. The state is literally defined by its mountains, rivers, and forests. Ever since I was a boy, I've been renewed by a walk in the woods. Discovering an unfamiliar plant, insect, or rock formation brings me joy. I geek out over lichen. Could I drop everything else in my life and become known as an expert on the great hikes of America? That sounds like fun except that I don't like to hike when it's really cold. Or when it's really hot. And I'm not in great shape so I avoid most hills. And I know nothing about hiking gear. So my content topic would be "The Middle-Aged Dude's Guide to Hiking Mostly Flat Trails in Mild Weather." There might be a small audience for that, but it's not going to help me achieve my life goals. And being known for middle-aged hiking would mean abandoning all the other things I'm good at, all the consequential skills I've accumulated for decades.

Boating and hiking are hobbies and passions, but do I want to be known for those things? Becoming known in the world today takes dedication and vicious consistency. Are these passions sustainable interests that will take me to the next level of my career? Is there a big enough audience to matter? No. Sometimes, a hobby is just a hobby.

Let's look at some other aspects of my life that might be more sustainable:

- I have more than three decades of life lessons from global business.

- I've had an extraordinary career. I've done just about every type of marketing job there is.

- I had the singular experience of studying under the famed author and consultant Peter Drucker for three years.

- I have an MBA and a graduate degree in applied behavioral sciences.

- I have the heart of a teacher.

Teaching people about digital marketing, and specifically the human-powered idea of marketing through social media, seems like a more sustainable interest than reading books on a boat. It's something I can be known for and something I truly enjoy. Even more important, it provides a sense of fulfillment. Knowing that I've made a positive change in a life is my fuel and my purpose.

This is another fundamental idea behind finding a place that will help you soar. Your sustainable interest must also be a concept that connects to the well-being of others. Sitting in a boat or discovering a new wildflower may be a passion, but teaching provides purpose. It's the glorious reward for all my hard work.

Without purpose, many will find it impossible to maintain an idea for months, for years, for a lifetime. For some, a sense of purpose dawns early, but for others, the motivation to serve becomes clear only after you get a response and feel the love from your new audience.

Instead of following your passion, sometimes your passion follows you. The passion shows up through the act of doing, achieving, and realizing that you're having a positive impact on people.

In Chapter 6, I give you an up close and personal view of James Altucher,[2] an extraordinary blogger and podcaster who has overcome a lifetime of setbacks to become known in the self-help world. James has interviewed dozens of the world's best-known leaders on his show, and he said they all exhibit one unifying quality: "Every person I spoke to wanted to solve a problem for the many. It doesn't matter how you give each day. It doesn't even matter how much. But everyone wanted to give and eventually they were given back.

"Nobody succeeded with just a great idea," he said. "Everyone succeeded because they built networks within networks of connections, friends, colleagues ... all striving toward their own personal goals, all trusting each other, and working together to help each other succeed. This is what happens only over time. This is why giving creates a bigger world – because you can never predict what will happen years later."

I hope the difference between a mere passion (centered on self) and a sustainable interest (centered on both you and others) is becoming clearer.

Standing for something

I'm blessed that one of my closest friends and collaborators, Tom Webster, is also among the wisest men I know. As vice president of Edison Research, Tom is continuously in a position to work closely with the powerful leaders of global companies and assess how they establish their authority.

"Being known is something more than just having top-of-mind awareness," he said. "You want to achieve top-of-mind *preference*. That's a more complex concept.[3]

"What's the first soft drink I think of? Well, the first one that pops into my mind might not be the soft drink I prefer. So having top-of-mind awareness is not the real goal.

"I believe the same concept applies for individuals and for being known. There are lots of ways to become famous. The key to success is to be known *for something*. You need to have a clear idea of what you want to be known for and to which significant body of people. This clarity influences how you present yourself, what you do, and where you do it.

"It's an existential question, beyond just a marketing question. What are you comfortable with, how do you see yourself, what is the space that you want to occupy in this world?

"Here's a story that makes my point," Webster continued. "A journalist called me to comment on an outlandish claim that was made on an infographic. It occurred to me that the claim, and the infographic, were produced by a person to extract this very thing – conversation in the press. *But the journalist called me.* The journalist trusted me, because I am known for truthful interpretation of data.

"Being known means standing for a thing. And over time, people will rely on you for that thing, they will count on you for that thing, they know you will never compromise on that thing. When you write something like 'Five Great Ways to Write 15 Lists of 10,' you're not standing for something other than pimping yourself for traffic. That's not going to create a lasting impression or matter very much over time."

The place that's right in front of you

I really love Tom's perspective and the idea of nurturing a personal brand that establishes *preference* and *meaning* over time. How can this happen for you? Sometimes this ideal is right in front of you, and all it takes is a spark to fan the fire.

Last year I worked with a talented woman named Betty Brennan, president of Taylor Studios ... a most interesting business. Her team creates detailed, historically accurate multimedia displays for museums. Over the years her business grew to the point where she was able to take over an old Wal-Mart site and fill it with a team that crafts prehistoric plants and animals, famous battle scenes, and historical panoramas of every kind. You have to love a business that maintains bins of dinosaur parts.

The Taylor Studios team employs extensive research and a multitude of multimedia techniques to relate a story about an idea, an animal, or a historical era. But Betty's business was stuck. There were only so many museums looking for her services, customer budgets were being cut, and her competition was fierce.

In Betty's mind, she was known for something very specific, but it was limiting her potential. "I make museum displays," she told me. "That's all I've ever done."

"No," I said, "you do more than that. You tell stories, but they're not on paper or in a video. You tell amazing stories in a physical space. You probably do that better than anyone in the world. You inspire people because you're the world's best physical storyteller."

I could tell by the silence on the other end of the phone that the ember of an idea was beginning to glow!

Reframing Betty's sustainable interest as "physical storytelling" created a more expansive and distinct identity that blended her life's work, talent, and purpose. The concept of applying storytelling beyond museums to businesses, universities, and sports facilities redefined how she wanted to be known in the world. Today, creating corporate "history walls" has become a growing part of her business.

The work we do together in the following chapters is meant to create these sparks in you and help you discover your "thing," as Tom Webster put it. I've selected battle-tested exercises to help you define your distinct place in the digital world and unearth your sustainable interest.

Perhaps, it's right in front of you, too.

CHAPTER 3

Finding Your Sustainable Interest

"Your vision will become clear only when you look into your own heart. Who looks outside, dreams; who looks inside, awakes."
– Carl Jung

It's time to roll up your sleeves and really get to work.

I've scoured the world for some "sparks" for you, and I've discovered seven fun and easy exercises to help you uncover your very own sustainable interest. I've used all these techniques in workshops and executive coaching sessions over the years, and they've never failed to move people in the right direction. There's bound to be one that works for you, too.

Finding your place, your sustainable interest, is step one in a four-step process. You don't have to complete all the exercises in this chapter, but I encourage you to try two or three that appeal to you. If you've completed the chapter and you're still struggling, don't worry. There are other prompts throughout the book that can get your juices flowing, and you can always come back to this part of the book later.

Let's rock on ...

Exercise 1: The "Only I ..."

This is my favorite way of getting a person focused in a hurry. Finish this sentence: "Only I ..."

That's difficult, isn't it?

As a busy person, you probably prefer to *do* instead of *think about* what you're doing and why. We normally don't spend time considering what makes us distinctive, but to become known, this discovery is critical.

Only I ... are you the most experienced, the most caring, the smartest, the most entertaining, the most trustworthy? Are you the best at service, at explaining things, at creating new approaches and ideas? Are you unique because of your education, the perspective that comes from where you live, who you know, or what you do? Why do your friends love you? What is it about you that keeps them coming back to your circle year after year?

Another clue to zeroing in on your "Only I" statement is the sort of questions people ask when they come to you for advice. Maybe this is a sign of what you're really known for.

I was mentoring a young woman and she told me that people were constantly coming to her for technical advice. "I can explain it really well," she said. "I can make complicated answers seem easy." I suggested that she needed to listen to these clues – people were helping her identify her strength, and perhaps her sustainable interest, through these questions.

If you can answer "Only I" thoroughly, accurately, and confidently, your path to becoming known will reveal itself. You'll know with certainty what you need to say, where you need to say it, and who is going to care about it.

Ann Handley, a wonderful author, speaker, and a founder

of Marketing Profs, calls this "Only I ..." concept your "rich thing."

"When I was eight years old," Ann said, "I wrote in my diary, 'I want to be a writter.' Even then, I knew I'd always need a copyeditor to help with spelling!

"Writing is my thing. But my bigger, richer thing is clear, compelling communication, period. Clear communication. Simple but not simplistic. Respect for the recipient. Regarding an audience as a privilege.

"Commit to your rich thing, whatever that might be. Lean into it. Learn it. Rub it all over your body and wallow in it, neck deep. Get obsessed with it. Go all in or no in. But realize, you're never 100 percent competent. The more you master, the more you realize you don't know. That sounds a little depressing, doesn't it? Maybe. Or consider the fun of discovering all those pools in need of your wallowing body. Consider the challenge of giving it your all."

Let's look at an example of how this concept can be applied.

One of my clients was facing a true business crisis. For years, she had been known as an expert in advising doctors on ways to reduce the overwhelming paperwork associated with malpractice insurance. But regulatory changes meant that this work was going away. No amount of effort or marketing would save her business and a reputation she had built over a decade.

I asked her to tell me what she loved about her job. How did she get into this business?

"When I was young," she said, "I nearly died from several complicated medical conditions. I'm only here today because of the doctors who saved me. So I want to give back. I want to help doctors any way I can."

Her emotion was rising as she described her true purpose. "It makes me angry that doctors face so much bureaucracy and paperwork today that they don't have time to see patients. I want to help them with that. I want to help doctors be doctors."

"That's it!" I said. "That's your 'Only I.' You don't handle insurance paperwork. You help doctors be doctors. That's your talent and your gift to the world. Aren't there lots of other tasks you could take on to reduce administrative burdens and help doctors be doctors?"

"Yes! There's so much more," she said. "That really is what I'm about. I could do that!"

Over the next few weeks, she scheduled meetings with the doctors in her extensive network and discovered a significant amount of new business opportunity. Just a month later she sent me a very kind email telling me that by more accurately defining her "Only I" and becoming known as "the person who helps doctors be doctors," she reinvented her business and was already looking forward to her most profitable year ever.

What are some of the steps you can take to better define your "Only I"?

Ask others. Every personal branding book will tell you to ask your friends about your talents and skills. But I find this to be limiting. Do your friends really see you in a professional environment? Will they tell you the truth, or what they think you want to hear? Will they draw their conclusions from events that happened years ago instead of what might be true about you today?

Instead of asking friends, I would go to people who have worked with you extensively and recently. Supervisors. Employees. Co-workers. Customers.

Don't do a survey. Have a long, significant conversation with them about what you want to do and where you want to go. Listen carefully for those keywords that will help define you in a unique way. Eventually you'll hear those words and think, yes! That's what I am and what I do!

Exercise 2: The 2 by 2

This is a simple yet powerful exercise that can help pinpoint exactly where you sit in your marketplace and where the opportunities for distinction might be. It's easiest to describe this technique through an example.

I had a client with experience in the field of adult education and self-improvement. But he was having difficulty focusing on how he was going to stand out because there were dozens of others writing about this topic. His first instinct was to focus on the emerging educational needs of millennials.

We determined that there were two important considerations in the continuing education market:

- **Age** – There are vast differences in how people learn, their subjects of interest, and the available time for learning based on their age. For example, a digital native in their 20s might naturally go to YouTube for content to improve their skills, whereas somebody in their 60s might have the time to enroll in a college class.

- **Cost** – The range of self-improvement cost options is dramatic. On one end, there's free educational content on the internet, and on the other end there's a master's degree that comes at great expense. And of course, there are many alternatives in between.

Because of the intense competition in the niche, it made sense to break down the competitive space to see if we could visually detect an opening. To begin this visualization, we determined that there were two important considerations in the continuing education market. We plotted this out and placed his established competitors on simple 2 x 2 chart.

Analysis of Continuing Education Bloggers

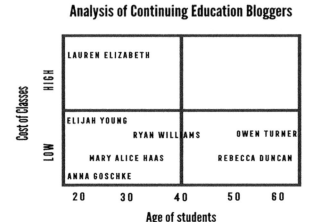

This analysis shows a crowd at the lower end of the market. Lots of people are creating content about low-cost continuing education options for every age group. Lauren Elizabeth has defined a nice niche for herself creating content for the high-cost end of the youth market.

But we also see an opening here, don't we? Nobody owns the topic of more expensive transformational opportunities for people over 40. My friend's initial idea was to address continuing education for millennials, but he switched his focus entirely because the topic represented by the upper right corner was uncontested.

Try this for your area of interest to reveal a topic you can be unique for you. Think about the two most important factors for your new target audience, and then plot them on a simple 2 x 2 chart. Nothing fancy. Just draw four boxes on a piece of paper.

You probably know your topic well enough to name two

important audience factors. The harder part, and the most important part, is doing thorough research to correctly place competitors in the appropriate box on the chart.

If you put the effort into it, there may be no better way to discover a sustainable interest than through this modest exercise.

Exercise 3: The Core Values Mash-Up

Jon Briggs had an incredibly successful career selling medical devices for a major corporation. He was at the top of his field before the age of 30. But he had become disenchanted with the pressures and ethical considerations he faced on a daily basis. It was time for a change.

And it happened quickly, in the most unexpected way.

He went to see his favorite American football team, the New England Patriots, play the Miami Dolphins and came across a fan wearing a hilarious t-shirt that had a cartoon depicting the iconic Dolphins logo diced up as sushi. As a die-hard Patriots fan, Jon just had to have it, and it planted a new idea. Could he create a business by becoming known as the "the anti-fan?" After all, poking fun at your competition is a great American sports tradition. But nobody seemed to "own" that idea in a big way.

He bought the rights to the humorous Dolphins logo and started creating new visual and video content that parodied famous sports franchises. Jon reached out to budding stand-up comedians to join the fun. Many of them were happy to step up to the challenge for the exposure. Merchandise sales fueled the cost of producing new content as Jon patiently built his brand.

In the completely saturated sports marketing category, doing the opposite of what people expected as an "Un-Fan" was a hit. By combining irreverence and sports, Jon ignited an untapped market. Within two months of creating his first parodies, his videos were receiving more than 200,000 views a week on YouTube!

"It's not exactly my passion," he said. "I'm not athletic, I'm not artistic, and I'm not funny. But I do love sports and I want to work in an environment that's fun every day ... and it is! It's something I can have fun with for years to come."

Jon created a sustainable interest by mashing up a personal value or characteristic (irreverence) with a crowded topic (sports) to create something new.

This is an effective strategy: Establish a distinctive presence by combining a core value with your primary interest or passion. Let's unpack this idea.

Here's a sample of common core characteristics and values:

Peace	Integrity	Environment
Wisdom	Love	Trust
Status	Friendship	Knowledge
Family	Justice	Reliability
Fame	Influence	Teamwork
Wealth	Happiness	Competitiveness
Power	Truth	Commitment
Authenticity	Kindness	Creativity
Joy	Spirituality	Honesty
Success	Loyalty	Fairness
Athletic/Fitness	Luxury	Independence
Humor	Craftsmanship	Design
Stylish	Charity	Education
Frugal	Building	Scientific

What are your core values? Are there any on this list that resonate with you? Can you mix and match these values – or others – with your topic to create a unique digital presence?

Let's say you love do-it-yourself crafts (DIY for short). Establishing yourself as someone who is known in the DIY segment would be exceptionally difficult because it's such a congested space. People all over the world are already creating quality content about their passion projects. So, you need to become creative with your interest or you'll get lost in the noise.

Let's look at the list of values and combine one of them with DIY to form something bold and new:

- DIY and Environment – This could be content devoted to finding the best way to complete your DIY projects in an earth-friendly way. How do you shop with low-impact? How do you repurpose leftover materials like bricks and plastic pipes? How do you build conservation, recycling, and space-saving into every project?

- DIY and Frugal – What if you created a blog or video series called "The $20 DIY Challenge"? Every project transforms an object, a room, even a landscape for just $20. You could even get your audience involved by asking them to submit their favorite $20 idea. I can think of a lot of sponsors who would be interested in that content!

Are you starting to see the possibilities? Don't be afraid of tackling an established topic. You simply have to find a fresh angle that will captivate your audience.

Let's try another topic, this time focusing on food. How many food bloggers are there? A bajillion. Really. I looked it up. In other words, this is a very, very saturated niche. To stand out you'll need to combine "food" with another interest or value.

Mash up food with the value of family. You love food, you love family, and you want to find ways to bring the family together while preparing a meal. What if you created a food site highlighting recipes that families could cook together? Everybody has a job, even the wee little ones will do some stirring and tasting. The whole family cooks a meal and then sits down to eat it together, without TV, video games, or text messages. Wouldn't that be a great concept?

Let's do one more. We'll combine food with humor. Oh, wait a minute! That one has already been taken by blogger and video star Fanny Slater, who has spent the past few years mashing up food and funny.

"From a very early age, I knew that making people happy – and especially making them laugh – was my purpose," Fanny told me. "I'm always trying to find a different route from the norm and that led me to acting and improv comedy as my first career. But after two years in Los Angeles, I found that I really didn't love that scene. So instead of being a comedian, I decided to search for another way to infuse humor into my work.

"Ever since I was a little girl, cooking was a big part of my family life. And as an adult, my passion kept bubbling to the top. I didn't pursue a culinary degree, typically what everybody else was doing, but I saw an opportunity to get into cooking my way (self-taught and not too serious) – maybe the opposite of the norm!

"Writing was a great outlet for me because it was one more way to be a storyteller and do it in my own unique voice. When I was in LA I started a blog with a food section and I began freelancing as a food writer on the side. My writing became increasingly popular and I attracted a significant social media following. I had found real happiness with a life that revolved around writing, food, and fun. It seemed to me that the next logical step was to apply these talents and create a cookbook.

"The cookbook idea was beginning to ferment when I received a message from my grandmother encouraging me to enter a cookbook competition sponsored by the television cooking celebrity Rachael Ray. I submitted a video, an essay, and three recipes. Five months later I was crowned the winner on Rachael's national television show."

Fanny's diligent work has continued to pay off – she's now a co-host of a Food Network cooking show.

"How did I become known in the crowded food business? My ability to make gourmet food approachable and funny is what draws people in. I don't take anything too seriously! Cooking deserves a certain level of respect, of course, but I love finding the humor in it too. Food should make you happy. I can make people laugh about a tuna melt and teach them something at the same time.

"The other factor that helped me become known is consistency. In fact, this may be the most important factor as you find your place on the web. I believe everybody has the potential to be known for something. It may take a while to figure out what that is, but it's inside everyone.

"Look at what everybody else is doing, and then do something else. Be the Fruit Loop in the bowl of Cheerios."

Exercise 4: Strengths Finder

The Gallup Company developed a simple and inexpensive on-line quiz called the Strengths Finder Test. More than 14 million people have taken this test, and for good reason – it is a remarkably accurate personality assessment! In essence, this exercise reveals your superpowers!

The test literally generates a report titled "What Makes You Stand-Out?" Seems like if you're trying to stand-out, that would be useful, right?

When I took this test, I found the results to be so detailed and precise that I was amazed. Here's a partial sample of the findings for me:

- You generate innovative ideas and propose systematic programs of action. You likely identify recurring configurations in the behavior of people, the functioning of processes, and the emergence of potential problems.

- You pay close attention to what is going on around you. You listen. You quiz people. You read.

- By nature, you work diligently to invent alternative courses of action. You notice new and unusual configurations in facts, evidence, or data. Others, however, can see only separate, unrelated bits of information.

- You automatically pinpoint trends, notice problems, and identify opportunities many people overlook.

- You are a sexy beast.

OK, I made the last one up. But if you've followed my blog, podcast, and books over the years, you'll know this report pinpoints me exactly, and these elements are central to my sustainable interest.

The report goes on to project the types of subjects and work environments that suit you best. The Strengths Finder is an irreplaceable method to discover the unique qualities you can bring to the world and to your content. It's a compass for your ultimate potential.

This process is powerful because it helps you realize that your unique place might have been right in front of you all along. Your sustainable interest might simply be … you.

Jane Hart has established herself as an authority on workplace learning and development. She's based in the UK and her influence is recognized throughout the world, making her in-demand as a consultant and speaker.

Hart's place in the world was determined through the simple awareness of her natural talents. She told me, "One of my clients described me like this: *'The vast knowledge you have – the way you scan, curate, see patterns and then write about it is such a gift.'* For many people, learning in the modern world is a complete maze, and they may flounder around trying to make sense of it all.

"My success comes from helping people make their way through that maze of new learning ideas, trends, tools, and practices. I wasn't always aware I had this strength. I knew I was good at assimilating a lot of information and connecting the dots, but I thought everyone could do that! Over the years, I've become more in-tune with this strength and I can see how valuable it has been in my success."

As my friend Sally Hogshead writes in her book *Fascinate,* "To become more fascinating, you don't have to change who you are. You have to become more of who you are, at your best."

Strengths Finder helps you accomplish just that because the first step is to be aware of who you are, at your best.

Exercise 5: The beautiful questions

Warren Berger wrote a useful book called *A More Beautiful Question*. In the book, he features the key questions of life that inspire and drive top designers, tech innovators, and entrepreneurs. Some of these questions might point to your sustainable interest. Try these on for size:

1. What is your tennis ball?

This question, derived from an MIT commencement speech given by Dropbox founder Drew Houston, is a good place to start because it cuts to the chase. As Houston explained, "The most successful people are obsessed with solving an important problem, something that matters to them. They remind me of a dog chasing a tennis ball." To increase your chances of success, Houston said, you must "find your tennis ball – the thing that pulls you."

I can relate to the tennis ball question. This obsessiveness is what drives me to write my books. Once I see a big problem people are struggling with, I can't rest until I figure it out.

Several years ago I had an exchange with a friend and we debated this question: Can anybody become known? Is there a standard process somebody could follow? I knew this was a big idea and I couldn't get this out of my head – for three years! My dogged search for an answer resulted in the book you're reading now.

2. What am I doing when I feel most alive?

What makes you shine?

What is the time and place where you feel most alive – whether it's when you're solving a problem, creating, connecting with someone, traveling, teaching, learning, or another activity? What is a sustainable interest that will allow you to do more of this?

I interviewed sociologist and author Martin Lindstrom, a remarkable man who can analyze small details in our lives to draw conclusions about our motivations. He said there are two places where people leave important clues about what makes them feel beautiful. First, he said every house has one room that's a statement about the person who lives there. It might display books, art, a musical instrument, collectables from travel, or family photos. This is an important statement about what you value. The "one room" in your house or apartment is probably apparent. What does this say about a possible sustainable interest?

The second place Lindstrom mentioned is your Facebook cover photo. He told me that this photo usually illustrates a place of importance and peace, a situation where you feel most alive. What do these places say about you?

3. What is something you believe that almost nobody agrees with?

This question from PayPal co-founder Peter Thiel is designed to do two things: help you figure out what you care about and determine whether it's worth pursuing. Thiel concedes that it's a challenging question because it can be tough to find an idea or belief that isn't shared by many others. Originality is deceptively difficult!

But if you can find a problem or challenge that no one else is tackling, it may be a place where you can sculpt your own niche and create value. "You don't want to be interchangeably competing with people," Thiel says.

Though we're taught to do what others are doing and try to succeed by out-competing them, in Thiel's view, this amounts to "beating your head against the wall – rather than going through the open door that no one is seeing."

4. What are you willing to try now?

One of the best ways to find your sustainable interest is through experimentation. Most people try to discover their purpose by reading books or taking self-help classes. But the "a-ha moment" may never come unless you actually try something through temporary assignments and moonlighting.

This was particularly helpful to me when I left the corporate world and started out on my own. I tried a few small assignments to test my business ideas in the marketplace. As I searched for my core business idea, I took on a few small assignments and found that I could succeed ... but I hated the work! Thank goodness I tested the idea first.

As a young man, I had always pictured myself being a college educator one day. During my corporate career, I started doing guest lectures at university classes. Then I did a few seminars for business owners. In 2008 I taught a marketing class at a community college, and I liked this well enough to commit to teaching at Rutgers University, which is some of the most rewarding work that I do.

5. What's your sentence?

This is a question designed to help you distill your sustainable interest to its essence by formulating a single sentence that sums up who you are and what you aim to achieve.

This is a variation of the "Only I" exercise. The idea is that a leader with a clear and strong purpose can be summed up in a single line. Here's "The Sentence" for a few famous people:

Mahatma Gandhi: "I am the father of passive resistance to create social change."

Abraham Lincoln: "I freed the slaves."

Charles Darwin: "I developed a theory of evolution to explain biological differences."

What would your sentence be? If your sentence is a goal not yet achieved, then how would your sustainable interest help you get there?

Exercise 6: Visualize your future

Close your eyes.

Imagine yourself two years in the future. Because of your achievements, you're a sought-after guest for podcast interviews. On this day, you're preparing for a show. Thousands of people from around the world will hear what you have to say.

What questions are you being asked on the podcast?

On another day in the future, you're backstage at a prominent industry event. You're about to take the stage as the closing keynote speaker. Anticipation fills the room as you're announced to the crowd. They can't wait to hear what you have to say! What topic are you speaking about?

You're still in the future. Many friends suggest that you write a book. You are known, and you are loved. "You've helped so many people," they say. "You should put your ideas down in a book!" This seems like a good suggestion. After all, nobody helps people quite like you. What is that special skill you need to share with others in that book?

OK. Open your eyes.

The first question I have is, how did you read the exercise with your eyes closed? Ha!

The next question is, what clues did you discover when you imagined your place in the future? Being known for something in the future doesn't require you to be an expert now. You have two years to get there. What's your plan?

Exercise 7: The 35 headlines

Now that you've explored these exercises, let's put your ideas to the test!

Think about the content you might like to create about your sustainable interest that will establish your authority and connect you to an audience. Are you thinking about blogging? Creating videos? Maybe a podcast?

Now make a list of the first 35 topics you'll cover about your idea. No need to get into details – just write down the headlines. For your content ideas, you might want to answer people's questions, provide your take on industry issues, and tell stories about relevant lessons from your career.

This exercise will provide two insights.

First, it delivers a perspective on how easily this topic will be to sustain. Developing an online presence takes time, tenacity, and consistent content. If you have trouble coming up with 35 ideas at the very beginning, you may need to rethink whether your interest is indeed sustainable over months and years.

Second, this exercise helps you refine your interest. I find that people who complete this list have no trouble with the first 10 topics. Maybe even the first 20 will flow easily. But when you get to the last 10 or 15 ideas, it takes some deep thought. Look at the entire list, from top to bottom. Is the theme consistent? When you get to the end, does your topic change at all? Do the last 10 topics help you refine or refocus your sustainable interest?

Your evolving "place"

Now that I've devoted more than 5,000 words in this chapter to help you find your sustainable interest, I need to shake you up with an important message: Don't obsess about it!

You may never truly know your place until you're into this process for a period of time. Your position will adjust and change and tune and sprout and flourish as you acclimate to your new role. Listen to your audience. You're going to learn so much along the way. Adapt. Adopt. Amend.

Chances are, you won't precisely identify your sustainable interest on the first try. But you're never going to move ahead and improve unless you begin.

Determining your place means overcoming the paralysis of self-doubt. The ultimate result of your work in this chapter doesn't have to be perfect. It doesn't even have to be correct. But it does have to be a start.

I love this story from author and speaker Dorie Clark. She explains how simply beginning and creating one single piece of content changed her life.[1]

"You may find that you have so many interests, it's hard to focus on just one," she said. "That was the problem I faced a number of years ago. I'd been working as a self-employed marketing consultant, and wanted to write a book – both to fulfill a long-standing personal goal, and also as a means of attracting new business.

"But the question of what to write about was tricky. In my consulting work, I was a generalist. I helped clients create marketing plans, social media strategies, messaging, and media relations. I used to work as a presidential campaign spokesperson and as a journalist, plus I'd run a nonprofit, directed a documentary film, and had been a theology student. It was hard to figure out what facet of my experience I should write about, and – critically – what would actually interest other people. What did I want to be known for?

"It was only when I started writing for the *Harvard Business Review* that my focus clarified. The second post I ever wrote was called "How to Reinvent Your Personal Brand" – a topic that interested me because of my numerous career changes. It wasn't necessarily meant to be my definitive statement to the world; it was just a 700-word blog post, out of dozens I'd done before.

"But for some reason, this one caught on. It received tons of comments on the website, and the editors asked me to write an expanded version for the *Harvard Business Review* magazine. Within a week of its publication, three different literary agents had reached out to me, asking if I'd be interested in representation. Two years later, my book *Reinventing You* was released, and I've subsequently lectured around the world about personal branding and professional reinvention.

"Sometimes you have to experiment with a lot of ideas and see which one sticks. If you're unsure, let the market decide.

Which posts receive the most comments, or retweets, or e-mail inquiries? What seems to capture people's imagination? Finding your niche is not an exact science, and you often won't know in advance what will work. If I had waited for the right idea, I'd probably still be waiting. Instead, I tried out a variety of ideas and, in the process, learned which one people cared about."

The important point from Dorie's lesson is, TRY. Think it through, do some self-assessment and research ... but don't become paralyzed if you're not 100 percent sure of what to do.

Becoming known is probably a multi-year journey. But the journey must start. You must begin, even if it's not perfect.

I hope by now your mind is spinning with possibilities. Are you starting to focus on your place? To complete the first part of your plan to become known, you should be able to name a sustainable interest that is:

- Aligned with your strengths

- Providing purpose because it benefits others

- About a distinctive topic that helps you reach your goals

- Inexhaustibly fascinating to you

If this is still hazy, don't worry. You can always return to this chapter, and there's more inspiration in store for you in the chapters ahead.

Sometimes the key to standing out is being in the right space. What space is right for you? Well, I thought you'd never ask!

CHAPTER 4

Step Two: Determining Your Space

"Our potential is one thing. What we do with it is quite another."
– Angela Duckworth, author of "Grit"

I'm a big fan of American baseball. I was only an average ball-player myself, but I adore the sport for its rich traditions, chess-like strategies, and colorful characters. One of my favorite personalities was a man who played near the beginning of the game's history, Willie Keeler.

At 5 feet, 4 inches tall, Willie was one of the smallest men to ever play professional baseball. In fact, his nickname was "Wee Willie." But when it came to hitting, he was a giant. In a game dominated by muscle-bound sluggers, the little hitter won two batting championships by perfecting a method to "slap" a ball into any hole left open by the defense.

When asked by a reporter how he became such a prodigious hitter, Willie replied simply, "I hit 'em where they ain't."

Willie's approach to hitting is also the recipe for finding a place to stand out on a very crowded web. You need to hit 'em where they ain't – you have to find that uncontested space and push your content through those holes with dependability.

In the quest to become known, finding your sustainable interest simply isn't enough if you can't present it in a channel that captures the attention of an audience big enough to make a difference. To succeed, you must have the perfect intersection of *place* and *space*.

In the last chapter, I helped you find your ideal *place,* what you want to be known for, and now you need to spend some time with this careful decision of *space*. Even if you're passionate, dedicated, and committed to the task ahead, your effort will end in frustration if the competition is so severe that you're never discovered or heard.

The first-mover advantage

The most obvious strategy for success is to be the first person to establish a foothold in a niche. Often, being first is more important than being the best!

An example of this "first-mover advantage" in action is Dr. Jamie Goode. There are thousands of people who write about wine, but Dr. Goode is one of the preeminent wine bloggers in the world, at least in part, because he was among the first to establish a presence on the topic.

"I was working as a science editor and I developed a great love of wine," he told me. "Then along came the internet and I was hooked as early as 1996. It was the cool thing back then to start hobby sites on platforms like Geocities. So I started a website called The New World of Wine, and this morphed into my website Wine Anorak. I began to blog in 2001 ... I believe I was the second person in the world with a wine blog!"

Dr. Goode's instincts to climb aboard the web early on served him well. Between 2001 and 2004, the number of wine-related blogs swelled from one to more than 700! If he had waited just one year to start his blog, it's likely he would have been swept away by the blogging typhoon, even if his content was superb. Today, there are tens of thousands of wine bloggers desperately trying to make a name for themselves. There are even annual conferences just for wine bloggers.

"I was lucky in that I arrived on the scene when there were far fewer voices out there," he said. "This enabled me to grow without a lot of competition. Also, I didn't have to make a living out of this at first, so that took the pressure off. If I were starting out now it would be much more difficult, but not impossible. It would take a tremendous amount of effort and some new point of differentiation to stand out."

By finding an uncrowded space, Dr. Goode was able to turn his pioneering blog, expertise, and distinctive voice into a lucrative career.

But he also understands that his first-mover advantage is vulnerable – the moment he stops being timely and relevant, he endangers his status. Consistency is his key to long-term success.

"To have an audience and a platform is not something I take for granted. I know how fortunate I am. I make a living from the wine blog, and I need to keep making a living, so this keeps me motivated! I have to pay my own way, and I work only in wine. For this sort of field – geeky wine talk – that enthusiasm means a great deal. If you aren't excited about something, then why would your readers be excited?"

The critical importance of the uncontested niche

So the obvious first step in finding your "space" on the web is determining if there are any still empty, or at least underpopulated, spaces left out there. And there are! Lots of them, in fact.

In the last chapter, you worked on finding your sustainable interest, and maybe by now you have an idea of what you want to be known for in this world. But before you start creating content on this topic, it's essential for you to know whether this effort will land on a big, wide runway with very little competition or a crowded little postage stamp-sized space where you may have no chance to connect with a meaningful audience.

I've been traveling around the world talking about the ideas behind KNOWN, and after one speech, a man came up to me and said, "I've been struggling to be known on the web for so long. I love what I do and I've created content on my subject for many years, but nobody's listening. Within the first 10 minutes of your talk I discovered what I was doing wrong – my space is entirely flooded with competition who have been doing this far longer, and far better, than me. It's clear that I need to refine my place and probably find an entirely new space."

The plan you'll have after completing the next chapter will help you avoid my friend's unfortunate fate!

Failing to find a meaningful, uncontested space is the primary reason people fail in their effort to become known.

To give yourself the best chance to succeed, you need to determine:

- Is your niche big enough to matter?

- Is it oversaturated already?

- Are there people who will be attracted to your sustainable interest?

Is it possible to find success even in an exceedingly crowded field like sports, food, fashion, or crafts? The answer is … maybe. I'll cover strategies to help you stand out and provide the best chance to become known even when the competition seems overpowering.

But first, let's go through a very simple exercise to determine the saturation level of your current space. Can you still be a first-mover on your topic, or will you have a battle on your hands?

Assessing your niche

If you have an idea of what you want to be known for – your sustainable interest – Google it. Think of some of the key terms that are associated with your identity and look at the search results. How much competition do you have?

If your search returns fewer than 500,000 results, this is extremely good news. You could be a true pioneer in this space. I know 500,000 sounds like a lot, but in a Google-view, that's nothing.

If the search returns between 500,000 and 1 million results, well ... you still might be able find success using some of the techniques in the next chapter. But it's going to require some patient work.

If the search exceeds 1 million results, that's a pretty saturated niche you're pursuing. You'll need to tweak it a bit or find a new angle on how you're thinking about your sustainable interest. *Note: Doing an analysis for a specific region of the world requires a bit more math, which can be found in Appendix II at the back of the book.*

Let me give you an example of how this analysis works. A friend called me and said he had an idea. He and his wife wanted to be known as the babymoon experts. Babymoon? I was unfamiliar with the term but learned that a babymoon is like a honeymoon right before you have a baby.

While he was talking to me, I did a Google search on the term – 316,000 results! Very promising. Not much content for that idea! I then did a search for "babymoon" on Google Trends, which provides a relative idea about the search traffic for a term. Over the past five years, there has been a steady rise in interest for the term "babymoon."

Not much content, rising interest in the idea ... my friend and his wife have a wide-open opportunity to become the king and queen of the babymoon world.

Here's another example. I've been working with a senior executive who wants to be known as an authority on succession planning. He's been a successful human resources executive for many years and is a true expert on the subject. But how crowded is the space?

If you do a search for "succession planning," you'll find more than 9 million results. Bad news? Not necessarily. This result shows there have been millions of *individual articles* about succession planning, but if you dig a little deeper, there's no one person or organization who "owns" the subject. Yes, this is a crowded niche. But my friend could establish himself as an authority for his subject because there's no other single person who is known for this topic.

But what if you're not as lucky as wine blogger Dr. Goode or the babymoon couple? What if you want to be known in a space that is VERY crowded like music or fitness or food? Is there hope? Yes, there is.

Just because you didn't start creating content at the beginning of the internet doesn't mean you can't be a pioneer. The world is so big that there's a chance for every person to find a sizable audience if you find the right place and space ... and commit to it.

Like Greg Kinman, for example. Greg is a retired middle-school English teacher from the rural community of Pleasant View, Tennessee (population 4,149). Better known as Hickok45, Greg is a YouTube sensation with more than 2 million subscribers to his channel, lucrative sponsorships, and paid appearances.

This is what he does on YouTube: He shoots guns. That's

all. He shoots old guns and new guns, brown guns and blue guns. He shoots bullets at gongs and pumpkins and watermelons and books and tanks full of water. Week in, week out, he is a grandpa who shoots. Occasionally he dresses like a cowboy if he wants to get a little fancy.

You might think this talent has the same entertainment value as the refrigerator repair channel or the "My Favorite Napkins" podcast ... but no! You get sucked into watching this guy's ability to blow things up at long range. A lot of people do. One of his videos has nearly 15 million views.

This example might seem outlandish, but it's actually sort of predictable. Greg has found his sustainable interest, he's found his space on YouTube, he's creating content with remarkable consistency (three videos every week for years), and he builds his audience through tireless engagement on his channel and public appearances.

If this retired school teacher can gun his way to the top, you can too, right?

I know it might seem daunting to carve your space when there is so much competition. But the truth is, the internet is just beginning. There is still room for you.

Author Kevin Kelly wrote in his book *The Inevitable*: "Right now, today, is the best time to start. There has never been a better day in the whole history of the world to invent something. There has never been a better time with more opportunities, more openings, lower barriers, higher benefit/risk ratios, better returns, greater upside than now. Right now, this minute. This is the moment that folks in the future will look back at and say, 'Oh, to have been alive and well back then!' The last 30 years created a marvelous starting point, a solid platform to build truly great things. But what's coming will be different, beyond, and other. The things we will make will be constantly, relentlessly becoming something else. And the coolest stuff of all has not been invented yet. Today truly is a wide-open frontier. We are all becoming. It is the best time ever in human history to begin. You are not late."

In the next chapter, I teach you eight different strategies to find the right space for you to occupy, even if you don't have a first-mover advantage:

1. Develop a unique content tone or point of view.

2. Move to a new social platform within your niche.

3. Dominate a content type.

4. Pioneer a new content form.

5. Differentiate through frequency.

6. Appeal to a new demographic target or region.

7. Leverage relationships with influencers.

8. Use curation as a strategy.

I'll go through each of these strategies in detail, and it's going to be mesmerizing, I assure you. We'll meet some remarkable people along the way and hear firsthand how these strategies operate in the real world. Let's go make some space.

CHAPTER 5

Eight Space Strategies

"I've always been in the right place and time. Of course, I steered myself there." – Bob Hope

Dr. Jamie Goode, our favorite wine blogger from Chapter 4, was a visionary (and maybe a bit lucky!) when he established his wine blogging space at the dawn of the internet. But most of us are not so fortunate.

"If I started now instead of 1999, I'm not sure the results would be the same," Dr. Goode said. "I'd be prepared to do something different. Everyone follows all the rules and ends up in the same competitive space. If you end up there, you're just one of a crowd. What can you do that's uniquely you? What will you be known for? Why would someone read what you write rather than the many existing voices?"

Why indeed?

Perhaps you can be known for how and where you tell your story. Let's go through eight different ways you can succeed by finding a workable space, even if you're not the first one on the scene.

1. Develop a unique tone or point of view

I started listening to jazz in a serious way when I was in college. I loved a weekly National Public Radio program that highlighted interviews with legends of the genre. One of the regular features of the program was a challenge: The host would play obscure recordings for the guest artist to see if they could name the musicians playing on the song. I was simply amazed that these experienced pros could correctly identify instrumental musicians – even the drummer! – by their "voice" and tone on a record! As I got older, I learned that I could also pick out some of my favorite musicians just by their unique tone, by the way they play – Pat Metheny, Ernie Watts, and Joshua Redman to name a few.

Like a brilliant musician, it's also possible for you to stand out in a noisy world by having a recognizable and distinctive tone. That's certainly been the case for James Altucher, the world's most unlikely self-help guru.[1]

The boyish, 48-year-old Altucher is a famously flawed entrepreneur and venture capitalist who spins tales of his greatest failures, breakdowns, and battles with severe depression. A few headlines will give you a flavor for his unusual blog:

- "Teach your kid how to kill people"

- "Why we should abolish the presidency"

- "Ten things the aliens forgot to tell us when they left us here"

- "Don't run over a baby in the middle of the street"

- "Murder, reinvention, and someone is watching you right now"

In the 1990s, James made millions as a young startup whiz. He lived in a 5,000-square-foot loft in Manhattan that he bought for $1.8 million and spent another $1 million renovating. He was rich enough to take a helicopter to Atlantic City on weekends to play poker.

But the lavish lifestyle didn't fill his emotional vacuum. "Nobody should feel sorry for me," he said. "I was really stupid, but I thought I was dirt poor. I felt like I needed $100 million to be happy. So I just started investing in all these other companies, and they were just stupid companies. Zero of these investments worked out."

To reclaim his wealth, he set his sights on conquering the stock market. He read more than 100 books on investing and eventually wrangled a job writing for investment blogs and *The Financial Times.* Before long, James's trademark hairdo, which looks like carnival cotton candy spun from steel wool, was a familiar sight on CNBC television.

But his fortunes crumbled once again during the world financial crisis that began in 2008. With few options remaining, he decided to chronicle his failures on a personal blog, which he named "Altucher Confidential."

On his blog, James routinely rips into sacred cows such as the value of college degrees, home ownership, and investing in the stock market. He openly writes about his failed mental health, relationship disasters, and how he lost millions of dollars (more than once).

His train wreck style of writing is so raw, so politically incorrect, so funny, and so deeply personal that you can't look away. "I just said, 'I've made every mistake in the book: Here's what they are,'" James said in an interview. And he discovered a sizable audience whose own dreams had just gone down the Wall Street sinkhole. "The number one search phrase on Google that takes people to my blog is 'I want to die,'" James said.

"I am an optimist," he said. "Basically, I've been down on the floor so many times, I know now that I can always bounce back, and it gets faster each time."

He's the anti-guru, a skinny, neurotic geek ... and that's refreshing in a Botox world of rah-rah cheerleaders and self-help high-fives.

After building his blog audience for several years, James wrote *Choose Yourself,* which he self-published on Amazon. The book sold more than a half-million copies and made *The Wall Street Journal*'s best-seller list.

Once James became known through his written content, he started an interview-style podcast and a career as a motivational speaker. On LinkedIn, where he publishes original free essays, he has a half-million followers.

James became known in a desperately crowded "self-help" field because he had the audacity to insert his raw and personal story into an otherwise predictable world of boring business advice.

"Advice is autobiography," he added. "I only say what has worked for me, and then others can choose to try it or not."

But becoming known through your unique tone or point of view doesn't mean you have to spill your guts to the world. Maybe it means painting yourself yellow now and then. At least that's the strategy of Isadora Becker, who leveraged her love of movies and media to become known as a cooking star in her native Brazil.

"I've been into cooking since I was a kid," she said. "I went to culinary school and my dream was always to give back and teach people about cooking for free. The whole YouTube thing was starting and I thought, 'why not me?'

"I've become known by combining my other interests to create an approach that is unique. I love movies, television, books ... all popular culture. The thing that makes me different is that I make recipes from famous food scenes in movies and TV shows and I dress up like the characters in the shows when I do the cooking."

Isadora's YouTube channel is sensational, red carpet fun! In one video, she paints herself yellow and wears a tall wig to become Marge Simpson, whipping up Homer's favorite do-nuts. In another, she prepares the famous $5 milkshake from the movie *Pulp Fiction*. She transforms into Walter White to make sky-blue candy that looks like something cooked up by the iconic *Breaking Bad* drug lord.

Isadora Becker as Marge Simpson in one of her popular YouTube videos

After building her video audience for more than four years, Isadora has diversified into other media. She has a cookbook of famous movie desserts and a television show based on the character-based recipes that made her known on YouTube.

"This was never just a hobby for me," she said. "I always intended it to be a business and to earn a living from becoming known. It's something that I love and a project I could do for a long time.

"No matter what happens, I won't stop making my videos," she said. "On the internet I can reach anybody. That was my original idea and my real purpose – to teach cooking for free, and I will always do that."

Finding the right "voice" for your content may not happen at the beginning of your journey or happen all at once. Your tone is forged through practice, feedback, and the occasional thunderbolt of inspiration.

It might be tempting to try to sound funnier/nerdier/hipper/snarkier than you are in real life, but that is likely to get exhausting. Your tone has to be a natural extension of your personality. James Altucher writes a quirky blog because he's quirky. Isadora Becker produces funny and creative videos because she's genuinely creative and funny. Finding a unique tone is about having the courage to let your freak flag fly!

James and Isadora had the mettle to adopt an outrageous approach and muscle their way to the top in very crowded categories. If you know your topic well, you probably already have an idea of the "voice" of other leaders in your industry. How can you insert your personality to stand out in an audacious new way?

2. Move to a new social platform within your niche

One of the first steps in your plan to become known should be a competitive analysis. Who are the other leaders in your field, and where are they publishing their content? Another strategy for success is to develop an audience in a fresh place that is underserved by your competitors.

Here's one of my favorite examples.

I live in the delightful city of Knoxville, Tennessee. It's a laid-back metropolis nestled in a valley between magnificent mountains and a string of gorgeous lakes and rivers. It's best known as the home of Oak Ridge National Laboratory, the University of Tennessee ... and apparently real estate agents. In our county of a half-million people, there are more than 6,000 licensed agents!

Becoming known among all that real estate noise might seem like a formidable challenge ... unless you're a young woman who stands out through a unique social media presence.

Suzy Trotta grew up in a family with big personalities and big business ambitions. A teacher by training, she was attracted to selling homes during the real estate boom of 2004.

"Traditional sales methods never appealed to me," she said. "Social media was the right channel at the right time. It allowed me to use my personality to attract business rather than selling on the same-old marketing platforms."

The field of real estate is notoriously social-media-spammy. It's a mystery, really. Real estate agents KNOW their business depends on relationships, but nevertheless their social media feeds are loaded with annoying open house announcements, price reductions, and can't miss fixer-uppers.

So while other realtors publish pictures of their "for sale" signs on Facebook and promote open houses on Twitter, Suzy posts pictures on Instagram of ... plastic donkeys. And ceramic cat planters. And the world's ugliest wallpaper. She created a hilarious and very human account by posting photos of all the outrageous stuff people leave behind when they "clean out" their homes for sale.

My favorite Instagram photo of Suzy's is her with a young man who is clearly so excited he is nearly jumping in the air. He has just closed on his first house. That's the kind of pure joy and celebration she features in her daily posts. That's how she differentiates her offering in a very crowded market and creates a significant emotional connection with her customers.

Why Instagram?

"Because a picture is worth a thousand words," she said. "I see so many things every day that most people wouldn't believe, or that just make me laugh out loud, and I HAVE to share it with the world. Twitter allows my audience to peek behind the real estate curtain, and Instagram pulls that curtain back even more!"

And the crazy pictures mean business. "I have a great client who originally found me through Twitter," Suzy said, "but we truly bonded over our cat pictures on Instagram. When he asked me to list his home, he actually emailed a picture of his cat (who is adorable). I have since sold his home and helped him buy two more. Because of Instagram, he knew I loved cats and that was important enough for him to hire me."

Suzy's social-media-driven star continues to rise, and after 11 years in the trenches she started her own agency. Now she's teaching her staff how to use social media to generate truly human connections. She attributes her unique online personality to her success in attracting real estate agents looking for a less conventional approach to business. "We don't actively recruit," she said. "The last nine agents we hired all found us online."

There are opportunities in almost every field to discover innovative ways to become known by connecting to an audience in new places. As the media world shifts, do you KNOW where your audience is today? Do your competitors?

3. Dominate a content type

A few years ago, YouTube published a research report showing that individuals and companies doing the best job building brands on their channel published three different types of content:

- **Hygiene content** serves the daily health of your audience. It gets people involved and helps them connect to you when they need you most because it answers common questions. Hygiene content is the most likely content type to turn up in organic search results, so it's great for building initial awareness. Examples of hygiene content are a gardening guide, a how-to video on fixing a flat tire, and tips on how to get in shape for ski season.

- **Hub content** is addictive content meant to keep your audience on your site. This could be a series of in-depth articles or an adventure video series that makes people want to stick around and learn more. The content may explore your values, your history, and your ideas. Hub content is so interesting that your fans want to "binge" to catch up on past episodes or delve into your archives if your content is written.

- **Hero content** is something brilliant, dramatic, and bold that transcends the normal day-to-day internet offerings. This content goes viral and demands attention. A famous example is the epic mini-movies Nike produces for the World Cup. Their blockbuster videos feature celebrity appearances and earn more than 100 million views on YouTube. Hero content doesn't have to be "Hollywood," but it's certainly more time-consuming and expensive to produce than your everyday video.

So another chance to differentiate yourself is to examine how these three content types are already being used in your niche. More than 90 percent of the time, your niche is probably dominated by hygiene content, and if that's the case, you've found an opportunity with a lot of potential.

Distinction through content type has made Rand Fishkin a celebrity in the very bland world of search engine optimization (SEO).

Before Rand came on the scene, the world of SEO was dominated by shadowy nerds who spent hours in private chat rooms trying to unravel Google's secret algorithms. The stakes were high, and the top players held their cards close to the vest.

Rand, the co-founder of software company Moz, overcame that image with a new kind of "hub" content that explained the secrets of SEO in a transparent and entertaining way. Standing alone in front of a video camera and a whiteboard each Friday, the hip "Wizard of Moz" repainted the gray world of SEO in wit and pastels. His videos propelled him to star status, and he's become a sought-after speaker and industry authority.

Like the other examples in this book, his success was an evolution, not a revolution.

"The white board videos were a happy accident," Rand said. "We filmed our first one simply because we happened to have a camera in the office that day. We put the video up on the blog, and it didn't actually resonate with our audience very much at all. But we had planted a seed of curiosity on our team about the use of long-form video – a content format that few in the industry had attempted.

"It took many years of practice to get any good at it, of course. There was a steep learning curve. We were doing the whiteboard videos for at least two years before they started gaining real traction and at least three years before the series became as popular as our regular text blog posts.

"Over this period we worked to get better step by step," Rand said. "We improved our cameras, our whiteboards, our content quality, and now it's regularly the winner in terms of our audience views and engagement.

"Putting myself out there and becoming known has definitely delivered a financial benefit to the business," he said. "Moz gets a little over 3 million monthly visits, and many of the folks who are active in our community become customers and advocates of our products. But it has also been interesting from the personal side. I have a definite need to produce things that help people and earn their appreciation. I like to say I've got a giant hole in my chest that can only be filled by the praise and thanks of others, and it drains like a sieve, so if I ever go too long without providing value to our audience, I feel empty and dried-up and awful."

A significant breakthrough occurred for Rand and his personal brand when he pioneered "hub" content in his industry. Is there an opportunity like that for you?

4. Try a new content form

One of the most crowded subject categories is digital marketing. There are thousands of people pumping out blog posts, videos, and infographics in an attempt to gain attention for their brands. How did Tom Fishburne find success in this saturated niche? By hitting them where they ain't ... in this case, cartoons!

Known as "The Marketoonist," Tom has become one of the best-known voices in his industry through his insightful and hilarious cartoons about business life.

"I often hear from people that they feel like I'm spying on them at work!" Tom said. "A friend of mine described my background as an example of 'the power of combinatory skills.' Putting two types of expertise together can give you a point of differentiation. In my case, I discovered that there aren't that many people with my background. There are plenty of cartoons about marketing, but not many that are created by a fellow marketer actually working in the field.

"To finish your sentence, ONLY I ... would be foolish enough to take out business school loans to become a cartoonist! I dreamed about being a cartoonist since I was a kid, but like many people, I shelved my childhood dreams as I got older. Ironically, it was only in business school that I started to think about cartooning again. I drew a weekly cartoon in the Harvard

Business School student newspaper. When my professor asked if I would create cartoons as teaching aids, I realized there might be something more to cartoons than meets the eye."

Tom's journey to become known required patience. After business school, he held traditional marketing roles at General Mills and Nestle. He continued to work on the side and slowly built an audience that was responding to his cartoons – and sharing them with their friends. "From my first cartoon in the student paper, it took 10 years to get to a point where I was ready to leave my day job," he said.

"As a marketer, my job was about trying to get engagement with people to buy boxes of our cereal, or whatever the product was. And I was suddenly finding people responding to cartoons. I started to think that with my marketing background, maybe there's something about this humble medium that could be used in this way."

Tom found his space by reviving a dying craft in a digital age.

Full-time newspaper editorial cartoonists are endangered – there are now fewer than 40 at American dailies, down from an estimated 200 in the early 1990s. And that total was 2,000 at the beginning of the 20th century, when there were many more newspapers in business.

It's ironic that a content form commonly associated with old-school channels like newspapers and magazines is so perfectly suited to the digital age. It just took somebody like Tom to figure that out.

"Cartoons are the original snack-able content," he said. "They convey a tremendous amount of information in a small space. And they're incredibly memorable, largely because cartoons communicate something unexpected for the humor to work.

"But what I like most about cartoons is that it's a participatory medium. Cartoons have words and pictures and the reader has to put the two together to unpack the meaning. That moment of figuring out what's going on in the image is pure magic.

"Today, many people are trying to find ways to connect with an audience through valuable content, but there's a wide span of what that content looks like. And if we're not careful, a lot of it ends up being more about quantity than quality. For me, there is only a focus on quality. That's how I earned my audience and the only way I'll keep it."

Quality cartoons helped Tom dominate a niche, but there are alternative content forms emerging on an almost daily basis. The pressure to find ways to stand out is constantly generating inventive new platforms.

An inspirational source of innovation is *The New York Times*. While traditional newspapers are failing everywhere, *The Times* seems to have turned the corner, in part because of the way they've embraced exciting new ways to display their content. In recent years, they've presented news and opinion pieces through highly engaging interactive graphics, immersive virtual experiences, 360-degree photo stories, and participatory quizzes and polls, to name a few.

The cost of producing these new content forms continues to drop – some can even be created right on a smartphone! Pay attention to the attractive and interesting new content forms emerging all around you and ask yourself, "Is this a format that could help me become distinctive and dominate my niche?"

5. Focus on frequency

To say John Lee Dumas is "known" and financially successful would be an understatement. Here are his own words on how he founded his "Entrepreneur On Fire" line of products by igniting his passion through exactly the right space based on frequency.

"The day I graduated from Providence College, I was commissioned as an Officer in the US Army. After a 13-month tour of duty in Iraq as an Armor Platoon Leader, I served for seven more years in the States – three active, and four in the reserves. After the Army, I set out to do what I was 'supposed to do'... find a JOB!

"I tried law school first. One semester was all I needed to realize law was not my calling. I headed home to Boston, where I accepted my first corporate job working in finance at John Hancock. I was dissatisfied with the corporate life and after 18 months, I quit and decided to see what the Big Apple had to offer. In New York, I worked for a tech startup, but I still hadn't quite found what I was looking for.

"I traveled far and wide in search of a sustainable interest, and I landed in San Diego, California, where I got into the real estate business. This was unfortunate timing – 2009 and the beginning of the recession, which hit California hard.

"In real estate, driving was a big part of my daily routine, and I needed some educational content that could help me pass the time in the car. A friend suggested that I listen to podcasts, to which I responded, 'huh?' I did some research, and it turned out podcasts were pretty cool. Free, targeted, on-demand content? Heck yeah!

"I listened to mainstream stuff at first, like National Public Radio. But when I started dabbling in the smaller shows, I realized something important. There are so many great podcasts out there, but none that offered daily episodes. With once-a-week shows, I was zipping through years of content in mere days, and I knew if I was experiencing this problem, others were too.

"I loved listening to interviews, and I also loved learning how entrepreneurs had succeeded in their niche. A concept of the perfect show – a combination of my passion and my interest – began to form. I wanted to tell the real story of an entrepreneur. Their failures, lessons learned, their AH-HA moments. I wanted to learn the steps they took to turn that moment of inspiration into success.

"Once I started the Entrepreneur On Fire podcast, there was no turning back. I thoroughly enjoyed every second of every day. Creating targeted, relevant content on a daily basis was feeding my passion for learning and storytelling. I started waking up earlier each day and working 12 hours without even noticing!

"My goal was to provide as much value as possible and hopefully gain followers and fans that were benefiting from the content I was providing. Here was my success recipe: Valuable Content, Consistent Content, Free Content.

"Before long, a community began to form that I lovingly refer to as Fire Nation, and they have guided me ever since."

Within two years John and his growing business were featured in *Forbes* magazine. He had turned his talent for storytelling into a hugely successful business that includes paid content, webinars, speaking, and consulting. He's making more than $1 million a year from his podcast-related line of products.

Let's break down this case study into the key elements.

John obviously had a passion for learning and storytelling, especially when it came to entrepreneurs. But that passion would have gone nowhere if he had not found the right space – a relevant audience that was big enough to make a difference.

Podcasting is a format that perfectly fit his personality and lifestyle (more on that in the next chapter), and by immersing himself in the audio world, he saw an opening: daily podcasts. Here was an open space for his message, an uncontested niche waiting for his voice.

Are you beginning to see the power of this formula?

If John had created another entrepreneurial blog, his message might have been lost. If he had written a book right away, his ideas may not have caught fire because without an established audience, who would buy it?

John started small and focused, connecting with an underserved daily podcast audience before diversifying into other content forms like blog posts, videos, and webinars.

On the other end of the content frequency spectrum is Avinash Kaushik of Google. Avinash only posts on his blog about digital analytics once a month, but it is a piece that is so breathtakingly epic that it commands attention, even in a crowded field. It's not unusual for him to deliver a 10,000-word post, a work that's about the size of two chapters of this book.

Perhaps one of the ways Avinash stands out is the *infrequency* of his posts. When something comes out, you know you need to pay attention!

6. Find a unique demographic or geographic niche

Another way to find an uncontested space is to think local. What topics can you dominate as a local or regional expert? You don't necessarily have to be the best in the world, just better or more knowledgeable than those around you.

How can you leverage your training, unique career path, and life experiences to bring a perspective that differs from others in your region? Are your local competitors taking advantage of all the ways you can create content and become known? Can you absorb an idea from another part of the world and pioneer it in your area?

One of my favorite examples of this strategy comes from a bright young guy named Juan Pablo Zurita.

A few years ago, I woke up to more than 1,000 consecutive tweets, some in English and some in Spanish, urging me to follow somebody called JuanPa. I figured this was spam or maybe Twitter had been hacked, but when I plowed through the endless messages, sure enough there was a tweet at the bottom of the pile from some guy named JuanPa: "Will you follow me back? I'd like to have a conversation with you," it said.

We exchanged notes over direct messaging and I asked him for an explanation of the 1,000 tweets. "I can't help it," Juan Pablo said. "They're my fans. They want to help me!"

As it turns out, the 18-year-old Mexican not only has more than a million fans, he also has a manager. When he reached out to me, the young man was already making quite a comfortable living by creating funny videos every day.

He wanted to ask me some questions about the future of the internet, so I invited him to have a Skype chat so I could learn his story. I discovered that Juan Pablo is a talented, grounded, and extraordinary young man with a vision of accomplishing much more in this world beyond an audience for funny videos.

Juan Pablo observed how young people in the United States were becoming YouTube-famous, but at that time, there weren't many stars from Spanish-speaking countries. At first, he began making videos in English to mimic his YouTube heroes. But he found that when he made Spanish videos, he received much more traction because there was far less competition. In fact, almost all of his followers spoke Spanish.

So he pivoted and focused on creating slapstick-style videos featuring cheesy teen humor and satires of famous Mexican personalities. He teamed up with a small tribe of emerging Mexican video stars to collaborate and share best practices.

"I think people feel emotionally connected to the videos," Juan Pablo said. "They live those same experiences and that makes a bond between us. And because the videos are so natural, organic, and looping … People really love them, and it gets to a point when they admire you. I think it's crazy! I still don't understand this phenomenon or how it happened but it has changed my life. My fans have helped me achieve a lot of important things in Mexico, and I love them."

Today JuanPa is an international star on YouTube and has even moved to traditional media like television. He's swarmed by fans when he walks down a city street (even in America), and his income from sponsorships exceeds that of his older brother, who has a degree in engineering.

"YouTube has become mainstream entertainment," he said. "I think there's a huge future there and I may move into other social networks as well. The key is to always be consistent and have an honest presence. I believe I can sustain a career this way. I'll probably go to college because I think following through on an education is important. By associating my college career with my internet career I believe I can do even bigger things in the future and have an unbelievable impact on people."

So even in the crowded market of teen YouTube stars, Juan

Pablo became known by focusing on an under-represented region like Mexico. This was also a key to real estate agent Suzy Trotta's success. She has no intention of becoming an internationally known realtor. The local audience of people in her sales territory is enough for her to achieve her goals.

If you can reach your goals by becoming known on a local level, focus on that as a point of differentiation.

7. Connect with industry influencers

Shawn Van Dyke was in a heap of trouble.

His wife had been diagnosed with multiple sclerosis. His job running a small construction company afforded a lot of flexibility, but it didn't provide the medical benefits he needed to cover his growing stack of bills or the salary level he needed to feed his five children.

"I was frustrated," he said. "The more broke I became, the harder I worked. The harder I worked, the more irritable I became. I was digging myself into a deeper and deeper hole financially, mentally, and even physically.

"I didn't like the person I was at home or at work and I knew something had to change. I had a few job offers but none of them worked out. In most cases I was trading one kind of insanity for another. I was at a loss about what to do with my life."

Talking with friends and a career coach helped Shawn get clear about his strengths. He loved the construction industry and sharing his business expertise with others. He sensed there was a huge need around teaching construction professionals how to run their businesses more efficiently. He needed something to work and didn't have a lot of room for error, so he decided to test the waters before committing his precious time to a new venture.

"I knew that most construction business owners start a company because they want freedom and a chance to build some-thing meaningful," Shawn said. "And they HATE paperwork, the most stressful part of the business. Before I started down the path of building a product, launching it, and then won-dering why no one was buying it, I decided to test my idea. I started a research project called the Skilled Trade Sound Busi-ness Project. The goal was to gather information about what they do, why they do it, and their challenges in growing their businesses.

"I was able to confirm that indeed, paperwork was the big-gest problem … and I also identified a host of other needs like HR management and job planning. I had enough ideas to de-velop a year's worth of content.

"To stand out, I did something crazy. I decided to write a book and give it away. It was a risk, but I thought this was a way to become known – by giving away extraordinary value.

"I needed to build an audience and chose Instagram be-cause I know how builders and makers think. They like to show the world their process, their work, their struggles, and the finished product. Instagram is perfect for that! Since I didn't have cool photos of projects to post every day, I started de-signing graphics that had short, positive tips from my book. I told them that the world needs craftspeople, and I expressed my respect for the work they do. I encouraged them to value themselves more, and I offered to help.

"Things started to happen. My free book helped me land a spot as a guest on a podcast. People were paying attention to me! Now my audience could hear my voice for the first time and my traction continued to grow."

But things were still moving too slowly for Shawn. He didn't have the luxury of building an audience patiently over time. He had medical bills to pay. He had mouths to feed. He needed to put a rocket behind his efforts, and that's the perfect time to engage with influencers as part of a personal branding strategy. When you don't have time to build your own audience, borrow someone else's!

We live in an amazing time when power and authority have been flipped. The seats of influence no longer reside behind a news desk, on Wall Street, or in the corner office. Today, anybody with an internet connection can create content and seize the opportunity to have a voice, create power, and find an audience.

Trusted influencers with enormous power to "move the needle" are emerging in every market vertical. And by paying attention to the people in his market, Shawn found a key influencer in the construction space.

"I had been following a well-known builder in Boston who had established a huge online audience," Shawn said. "He was doing great work and was obviously spending a lot of time connecting to people on Instagram and Snapchat. I looked for opportunities to engage with him by commenting on his posts for a few months. I felt sure he knew who I was, so I took the next step and asked him a few questions over email. That went well, and it led to a follow-up phone call. So I was building on this weak social relationship from the internet and I was becoming a real human being to him.

"As popular as he was, I could tell that he had opportunities to improve his business. In the spirit of creating amazing value, I offered my consulting services to him for free, with no expectation of getting anything in return.

"I was providing so much great value to him that he started talking about me on his social media accounts. He reposted pictures of my advice and labeled me as 'his coach.' That was the validation I needed! My social media audience exploded all at once.

"This worked so well I identified a few more influencers in the construction space and invited them to a private Facebook group. My connections in this group led to my first invitation to speak at a national building supply show. All of this opportunity came about because I was genuinely helping people. My content isn't about selling me. It's about serving others."

Shawn probably didn't know it, but a large part of his success was due to a psychological principle called *reciprocity*.

Humans have a deep psychological need to repay a debt or kindness. If somebody gives you a gift, you probably look for an opportunity to return the favor. If a couple invites you to a party, you probably feel a little guilt until you can invite them to something in return.

This deep-seated need for reciprocity is so powerful that after intensive study, sociologists such as Alvin Gouldner report that there's no human society that does not subscribe to this rule.

So when Shawn provided his consulting services for free ... well, something HAD to happen. In return, the famous builder promoted Shawn and his work, an event that led to more exposure and his first speaking invitation. Shawn scaled this by offering free services to the influencers in his Facebook group.

This first success began a cycle of generosity and reciprocity that rapidly made him well-known in his industry. Shawn began turning up on lists of the most influential people in the U.S. construction industry. He probably could have earned this recognition himself with many years of work, but the golden touch of his influencer connections helped him advance his timeline.

This story has a happy ending.

Focusing on becoming known for his construction business expertise freed up time for Shawn to spend with his family. His priority is creating family experiences and enjoying memorable events before his wife's terrible disease worsens. The momentum of his brand is building, the money is starting to come, and the stack of bills is getting smaller ... because Shawn is known.

"The most encouraging part of this for me has been receiving messages from people who tell me my advice has changed their businesses, and their lives. My fuel is knowing that I am making a difference."

Connecting with influencers can have a profound impact on your success. I'll cover this in more detail in Chapter 7 when we look at ideas on how to build your audience.

8. Use curation as a niche

Here's a common problem for almost everybody: We don't have enough time to digest the universe of information available about our favorite topic, profession, or hobby. One of the ways to stand out, especially in a saturated space, is to help your audience cut through this information overload by summarizing the most significant articles in a regular post.

This is a technique called *content curation*. It's an interesting strategy because if you do it well, you may have no competition! Typically, every topic needs only one curator, and if you're first on the scene, you'll own the niche.

Curation can also be an effective strategy if you lack the time or talent to create original content of your own.

Here's an example of how this approach operates in the real world. While working on a client project, Christopher Korody got hooked on drones. Although this is an emerging technology, there are already many useful applications for drones and a rapidly growing fan base of passionate hobbyists.

Christopher established first-mover advantage without creating a single piece of original content. He's become an industry authority by curating helpful drone-related news on his site every day. He has become so well-known that he has created a drone-related consulting business based on his new expertise.

Similarly, Scott Monty established himself as an important voice of authority in the over-crowded digital marketing space by publishing a weekly newsletter, "The Full Monty," devoted to summarizing important developments in social media, content marketing, and advertising. The publication is entertaining as well as informative because Scott adds his own witty commentary to his news summaries.

Content curation is also a popular strategy in regulated industries such as pharmaceuticals, banking, and insurance. Creating original content in those industries can be difficult and expensive, but curating articles from other sites is less risky. In the health field, for example, there are curation sources for news on diabetes and other diseases, establishing the newsletter's author as the authority in the industry even if they're not generating any original content of their own.

But curation involves more than just listing popular industry headlines. It's serious work. Here are a few best practices if curation sounds like an option for you:

- Use content from a variety of sources and platforms, and help your readers discover new sources of news.

- Add your own voice by occasionally including a comment or opinion with a news item.

- Commit to consistency. Once you've established a publication schedule – daily, weekly, or monthly depending on the topic – keep to it. You want your readers to depend on you.

- Use curation tools. You probably already have some favorite sources, but there are a number of apps out there like BuzzSumo and Feed.ly to help you streamline the process.

Throughout this book, I've talked a lot about content, and it's time to get into this more deeply. The third step on the path to become known is filling your new space with content. What kind of content is exactly right for you? It's time to find out!

CHAPTER 6

Step Three: Finding Your Fuel

"Be so good they can't ignore you."
– Steve Martin, comedian, author, banjo player

By now you've detected a theme that has bobbed and weaved through every chapter and case study: Content is the fuel that makes all of this happen.

If you're a politician, famous athlete, or Kardashian-esque celebrity, you get a free pass. You can skip this chapter. In fact, you can skip the whole book. But if you're a normal dude or dude-ette, you'll actually have to create something to become known. As you climb your way to the top, the rungs of the ladder are content.

For many, this is the point where I'll lose you. You'll put down your latte, softly close the book, and sigh, "I can't write." Or maybe, "I simply don't have time for this."

Please. Breathe deeply, take another sip of your latte before it gets cold, and hang with me for a few minutes, OK? Here are the questions I'll answer in this chapter, and I think if you keep reading it will calm you down ... and maybe even pump (clap) you up.

- What specific type of content helps you become known?

- What kind of content is exactly right for you?

- How do you find the time for this?

- How do you start?

Those are the questions on your mind, right? See, I know you.

The information available on creating, publishing, and promoting content could fill countless books. I had to decide how far to go down the content rabbit hole, and this was my guide: If you need information that's readily available on the web – like how to set up a blog or podcast – I'm not going to cover it here. My job is not to replace Google. I'm trying to open your eyes and poke your brain in helpful new ways. Besides, whatever I tell you will be out of date as the tech changes, so trust me, Google is your friend when it's time to get into the crinkly details of setting up your content platforms.

< END OF WARNING >

It's now safe to return to our regularly scheduled program. Let's tackle these big questions about the role of content and your personal brand.

What type of content helps you become known?

I'll tell you a little story to spell out the answer to this question for you.

A few years ago, I wrote a somewhat controversial post

about a new trend called *influence marketing*. Today, this is a mainstream idea, but when I wrote the article in 2011, it was an entirely new concept. The post attracted a lot of attention. It was shared on the web nearly 2,000 times and had comments from dozens of readers who thought the idea was either exciting or despicable.

The attention this article received sent signals to Google that the post was something special in the new and uncontested niche of influence marketing. It started quite a chain reaction.

Three weeks after I wrote the post, a reporter from *The New York Times* called and told me she found my blog through a web search. She was conducting research for an article on this new marketing trend and asked if she could interview me. A few weeks later, four of my quotes appeared in an article in the Sunday edition of *The New York Times,* the most-read edition of the most-read daily newspaper in America.

But wait! There's more! The article was syndicated, meaning it was carried by other newspapers across America and around the world. The *Daily Mail* in the U.K. took quotes from this first article and created an entirely new piece ... that was then syndicated and also began to travel around the world.

Overnight, I became known as the go-to expert on influence marketing. This eventually led to a publishing contract to write the first book on the subject (*Return On Influence*) and invitations to speak on the topic all over the world. I even landed a consulting assignment to help an advertising agency in Japan establish an influence marketing department.

And this success was initiated from just one blog post.

Let's dissect this story. What was the role of content in helping me become known?

The key to success is "rich content"

Think about this: Would I have been found by that reporter from *The New York Times* if I had only posted my ideas about influence marketing on Facebook? On Twitter? On LinkedIn?

The answer is obvious – no. It's improbable that content from those sources would turn up in the first results of a web search. The reporter found my post because it was a significant piece of public content.

To have an opportunity for real authority on the web and vast reach, you need a certain type of content that has the depth and breadth to be discoverable. To be known, you need to focus on one of these four types of "rich" content:

- **Written content like a blog**: Blogs are easy and low-cost to start but can be time-consuming to maintain. They're a primary contributor to search engine ranking success and an excellent way to build thought leadership and community.

- **Audio content like a podcast**: A podcast is an internet-based radio show. Anyone can start their own program today. A study by Edison Research showed that podcast listeners are more loyal, better educated, and wealthier than other online audiences. The cost of maintaining a podcast can be moderate to high, depending on frequency.

- **A video series**: This content type is excellent when you need to entertain, demonstrate, and teach. Engagement levels can be high, and video is especially popular with younger audiences. The cost and complexity of produc-

ing videos for YouTube can vary widely from live streaming to complex productions.

- **Visual content:** Infographics, illustrations, and photo-
graphs are ideal if you're building an audience on Facebook, Instagram, or Pinterest. They attract a lot of social-
sharing and typically can be produced at a reasonable
cost.

Only high-quality, conversational content from at least one
of these sources will provide the fuel you need to stand out and
become known.

A little later in this chapter I'll give you some tools to help
you narrow down these choices and pick the right content type
for you.

Content is Google's best friend

The second reason that my post on influence marketing helped
me is because Google liked it.

In our journey to become known, we need all the help we
can get, and one of the best advantages we can ever hope for is
an assist from Google. In fact, without that vital search engine,
the reporter never would have found me and my mini-career
in influence marketing may not have happened. This is why
you always want the Google juice to flow in your direction.

Search engine optimization is a $30 billion industry that
is complicated and ever-changing. But there are a few things
about SEO that can explain how my blog post worked for
me. Here are some of the factors that go into the search
algorithm:

- **Age and size of site:** By the time my article was published,

I had been consistently creating content for more than four years. If it had been the first article I ever posted, it's unlikely Google would have noticed me. This is one of the reasons it may take months or even years to build momentum for your personal brand – Google looks for consistent quality over time.

- **Backlinks:** I'm sure you've clicked on a link within a post that leads to a related article. This is called a *hyperlink* or *backlink*. When another website links to your content like that, it's a signal to Google that your content is noteworthy and respected. The number, quality, diversity, and relevance of incoming links is extremely important to search success. That's why spending the time to produce excellent content is a good long-term investment. Quality content will eventually attract links from other publishers.

- **Dwell time:** Google likes it when people stick around on your content, which is known as *dwell time*. If someone finds you through a search, visits your site, and then immediately goes back to Google for another search, it's an indication that Google didn't deliver what its search customer wanted. In my example, once people found the influence marketing article, they stayed and read it. (And it was lengthy, so they stayed for a while.) In the eyes of Google, this was a positive sign that the post delivered the goods.

This is a very high-level view of content's impact on search engines. There are a lot of specialists and resources out there to help you as you progress on your journey, but this provides a glimpse into the Google world to explain how the influence marketing article worked for me and how content can also work for you.

Selecting a source of rich content and publishing consistently is something you MUST do to be known today.

The next question is ...

What kind of content is right for you?

You need to choose one of these forms of rich content and stick with it for a while. But you may look around and see competitors trying to do everything – podcasts and eBooks and Facebook and Twitter and Snapchat and on and on and on.

Can you sustain that? No. You're one person, and you probably don't want to spend your whole life creating content ... so pick one form, do it really well, and build your audience there for at least a year or so. Resist the temptation to do everything and be everywhere. Focus, focus, focus on one thing, and learn to be excellent in that space.

Which source of rich content should you choose? Here are three considerations.

1. Find the open space

Once again, the first consideration is to "hit 'em where they ain't." In some respects, your choice might be made for you. Take a hard look at the content being produced in your field of interest. Try to get a sense for the uncontested spaces, and determine if there's an under-served content opportunity there. And then ... go for it!

2. Figure out what you love to do

Ever since I was a young man I loved to write. When I was in high school, I had a job reporting for the local newspaper, and I eventually majored in journalism. Writing is my natural choice for rich content, and I've been happily blogging for nearly a decade.

I migrated to a content form I love. Yes, the competitive

landscape is an important consideration, but if you don't love what you do, you're going to quit – and I don't want you to quit! You may be spending years creating content, so you should love what you do, first and foremost.

3. Match content and personality type

One of the content channels I like but never really embraced is Snapchat. I couldn't figure out why it "wasn't me" until I saw a blog post that said the most successful people on Snapchat are goofy and random. Maybe that explains it. I don't think people who know me would describe me as a goofy and random guy.

I think content platforms can match to specific personality types, and this is something to think about when deciding what's ideal for you.

Between the slow, cerebral demands of blogging and the in-the-moment improv of Snapchat is a continuum of content options for the range of human personalities. Here's an overview of how content might match with personality.

Content forms more likely to appeal to introverts:

- Blogging

- Writing books

- Webinars

- Visual content like Pinterest, Instagram, and infographics

- Slide presentations

- Podcasts where you interview other people

- Videos where you interview guests

Content forms more likely to appeal to extroverts:

- Snapchat

- Live-streaming video

- Solo videos

- Solo podcasts

- Twitter chats

There's also a connection between personality and where you distribute your content.

Some platforms are prone to a lot of audience engagement and comments, whereas other forms may be quieter.

"Quiet" platforms that might appeal to introverts:

- Podcasts distributed on iTunes, where there is very little feedback

- SlideShare – A free site owned by LinkedIn

- Pinterest – A popular platform where you "pin" favorite visual images to your boards

- LinkedIn – A publishing platform with largely "professional" engagement

- Instagram – A photo site where most engagement is typically in the form of "likes"

- Twitter – Distributing links to your content is relatively easy and normally doesn't attract the commentary it once did

Platforms with more active engagement:

- Snapchat – Part of its popularity is the high engagement level

- Blogging – Your content and audience determine the engagement level, which could be lively or quiet

- Facebook – It's easy to leave short comments and sometimes it can get out of hand!

- Facebook Live or other streaming video – Attracts a lot of in-the-moment, random comments

By thinking through *what* you publish and *where* you publish it, you can create a plan that's most likely to fit your personality.

I want to emphasize that I'm not trying to pigeon-hole people. We are diverse and lovely as we are. There's absolutely no reason why a shy person can't enjoy posting on Snapchat and a chatty person wouldn't love stirring things up on a blog. These lists simply provide some food for thought.

If you're unsure of what might be the best fit for you, experiment with a few different platforms and discover something you love.

How do you find the time for this?

Throughout this book you've seen dozens of examples of people who have become known in their industries, fueled by their content. Here's a fact: They have the same number of hours in a day as you. Everybody has the same time to create content, but not everybody makes it a priority. The real issue isn't having the time, it's having the tenacity and drive to do it ... and keep doing it.

There's probably nothing I can write that can impact your determination, but I can provide you with 20 ideas to help you squeeze more content-producing productivity out of every hour:

1. Make time to create.

Block out several undistracted hours each week to create. Schedule this time with discipline, like you would prioritize an important meeting.

2. Add an insight.

Let's say you see a post of five ways to bake a better cake. For your cooking blog, create a new post noting the original article and writer, list the five ideas, and then add two more ideas of your own. You've just added value to your readers, helped the original author by linking to their content, and created a great piece in a fraction of the time.

3. Find a routine.

Create content at your most productive time each day or on the same day each week. When it becomes your routine, you might even look forward to it.

4. Let it sit.

Don't spin your wheels for too long on any one idea. If you're feeling stuck, move on to another project to use your time productively.

5. Take a break.

Taking breaks saves time in the long run. Studies show that even two-minute breaks can increase productivity by 11 percent.

6. Imperfect is perfect.

The biggest obstacle for many people is wasting too much time in pursuit of perfection. You're human. It's not going to be perfect. Push the publish button any way.

7. Use the apps.

There are free apps to help you create illustrations, infographics, and videos. You can create podcasts on your smartphone now. There are apps to help you find content ideas, guide your SEO, and write better headlines. Use them.

8. Mix the media.

Don't have time to write a post this week? You can make a three-minute video in ... well, three minutes! Embedding a video in a blog post is an easy time-saver, and it provides variety for your readers.

9. Get a little help from your friends.

In a time crunch? Invite some of your trusted friends to submit a guest blog post, a video for your channel, or a "takeover" of your Instagram or Snapchat account.

10. Learn to say no.

Every minute you spend on tasks not central to your goal is time that is gone forever. Guard your time carefully – it's the only asset you have to devote to content creation.

11. Outsource the admin.

Much of the time required to create content is spent on editing, producing, and scheduling. Podcasting and video editing can be particularly time-consuming. Outsource these tasks so you can spend your time on the actual content.

12. Don't multitask.

Turn off the TV, smartphone, iPad, text messages, and alerts. An average knowledge worker wastes 28 percent of their time on interruptions and "recovery time."

13. Prepare a content calendar.

Plotting out your content week by week can help you visualize your commitments and arrange your content to align with your work and vacation schedule. For example, I don't schedule content that I expect to attract high levels of engagement on days jammed with meetings.

14. Create round-up posts.
Come up with an interesting question or industry problem, and ask a group of friends to provide a two- or three-sentence answer. Collect them all and you've curated an extremely interesting post with minimal original work on your part.

15. Set a deadline.
When I was starting out as a blogger, it took me forever to create content. I fretted over so many details. I found that when I set time limits on the content (I will spend one more hour on this – then publish!), I was much more effective.

16. Don't overthink it.
A great piece of content doesn't have to be a PhD thesis or contain earth-shattering insight. Some of my most popular posts have emerged from a simple observation or a question from a friend. There's no pressure to be profound.

17. Tally your time.
Keep a record each week of the total hours spent in a state of unbroken concentration. This technique provides concrete data about how much deep work you actually accomplish, and the embarrassment of a small tally motivates a more intense commitment to focusing on your content.

18. Repurpose your content.
Transcribe a podcast to create a blog post. Use ideas from a blog post to publish a slide presentation. Base an infographic on your slide content. Starting to see the potential? It's possible to make many pieces of content from one core idea.

19. Narrate.

Most people can speak at least three times faster than they can type. I hire a college student in my area to transcribe all sorts of audio and video content, which saves a significant amount of time. There are also apps available that can do a decent job of transcribing at very low cost, or even free.

20. Drink a beer.

Several research studies showed that slightly elevating the alcohol level in the bloodstream increases creativity. I am not making this up. It might be the best tip in the whole book – maybe the best tip on the entire planet. No need to thank me.

Now that you've found a content type and the determination to do it, you might be wondering ...

How do I start?

Committing to this path might seem intimidating, but remember, greatness is doable. Greatness is an accumulation of many, many individual feats, and each of them is achievable. To be known, you must have the courage to begin and the constancy to endure.

Perhaps you're struggling with legitimate fears like:

- Lack of confidence in your skills

- Fear of negative comments or people harassing you

- Finding enough ideas for your blog, video, or podcast

- Being intimidated by the technical aspects of creating content

Let's address each of these fears, one by one.

Lack of confidence in your skills

Broke, unemployed, embroiled in a divorce, $50,000 in debt, losing his business … Australia real estate executive Jeff Bullas was in the midst of a miserable period in his life a few years ago.

"You could say I had some time on my hands all of a sudden," Bullas joked. "But it turned out to be a time of reflection and personal growth. I spent a lot of time exploring the Internet, trying to determine my next step. This was a time when social media was getting popular and I noticed how people were obsessed with Facebook. I became curious about what this meant for businesses in the future.

"I came across a blog post that said, 'even if you only have an inkling of what you want to do, just start.' So I did. I had nothing to lose and I was intrigued by this idea that I could write something and connect with people from all over the world. I wanted to know what that would be like.

"I had no grand plan, no business scheme, I wasn't even a good writer at first. In fact, I was terrible! If anybody thinks they can't blog, I tell them to go back and look at my early posts! They would be horrified. But there are a lot of resources out there to help, and with some determination, I learned to be a better writer."

Today, Jeff has one of the top marketing blogs on the web and has built a loyal audience that's enabled side projects in consulting, coaching, and online seminars.

"Blogging literally change my life," he said. "It was brutally hard at first, but it has become a source of real joy for me now. I have a global forum to share my ideas, and I've made some of my closest friendships through my site."

The great thing about creating content is that you really do get better with practice. And if you can't write, you can try making videos. And if you don't like videos, you can give it a go in audio by creating a podcast.

One stumbling block is that some people simply lack the creative gene and don't enjoy creating content. And if you don't like creating content, you're going to suck at creating content. In that case, it's time to get help.

I have a friend who hired a writing coach and editor, and now he's turning out some great stuff. I can point to at least five well-known social media stars who don't write their own blog posts. In fact, they don't write their own books.

But they've found a way to publish. Is that misleading people? Not if it's done well and with integrity. When the leader of a country gives an important speech on national television, he probably didn't write the entire speech. Is it his? Yes. When a CEO writes a letter to shareholders in an annual report, did she write it? No. Is it hers? Yes.

Getting help for your content makes good business sense as long as:

1. The ideas are yours.

2. You're accountable for every word.

3. You never mislead people, including having somebody "engage" for you or lying about the fact that you get help.

Fear of negative comments

You're not going to make everybody happy all the time. You're not pizza.

If you put yourself out there, it's likely that people will disagree with you now and then. You might love to challenge and debate in the safety of your own home or when you're with friends, but putting it out in public is another matter. This is a legitimate fear, but it's also a surmountable one.

The first thing to know is that it's extremely unlikely that people will be mean to you or criticize your content efforts, even if you make a mistake (and I'm living proof of this!). In general, people who take the time to connect with your content will be kind and supportive ... amazingly so.

I've received more than 60,000 comments on my blog {grow}. Here's how many comments I've deleted because they were either overly harsh or threatening: nine. That's a percentage so small that it's not even worth thinking about.

People might debate your point or challenge you, but that's part of the fun and something to embrace. Every day, the comment section on my blog is like a party. People show up and leave me their little gifts from all over the world.

As the light of your personal brand begins to shine brighter, it's possible that you might eventually attract a negative comment, like a moth to the flame. You might even regard that as a positive sign of progress – you now matter enough for somebody to be a jerk!

Negative comments can hurt, but it's also an opportunity to show what you're made of. Here's a strategy to address the problem in a professional manner:

1. Acknowledge their right to complain or have a differing opinion. Show empathy and try to defuse the emotion by saying something like, "Thank you for your dissenting view. I appreciate that you took the time to express an opinion." About 98 percent of the time, this takes care of the problem because most people just want to be acknowledged.

2. Apologize if warranted. And, maybe even if it isn't warranted.

3. Resolve the issue on the spot if it's a simple misunder-standing, or offer to take the issue offline through a phone call or email.

4. If the problem persists even after you've been kind, it's time to abandon the issue and perhaps block the person if they're being unprofessional.

If a person leaves a truly hateful or threatening comment, most platforms like a blog or Facebook provide an opportunity to delete it. Another technique I've used is to say, "You know, I think you make a good point here. I'm just disappointed you had to be so mean about the way you said it." The response is usually, "I'm sorry. I didn't intend to come across as mean."

Don't hesitate to start creating content because you're afraid of negativity. If you're a good person sincerely trying to help and teach others, negative comments are almost never a concern.

You don't know what to say

At one time or another, everyone faces writer's block (YouTu-bers block?). Your mind is blank. What are you supposed to say?

In every waking hour of your day, ideas are streaming over you like a waterfall. You're just not conditioned to notice them. In fact, you probably tune them out.

Becoming a consistent content creator means being alert and considering the entire world as a source of inspiration. Once you "tune in," an idea might grab you in an article you read, a speech you attend, or something you hear on the news.

Creating content takes discipline – not just in producing it but in constantly collecting ideas. The way to always stay fresh is to **view your daily life through the lens of possible new content.**

Here are examples of how tuning in to my environment led to great content ideas:

- While preparing for a speech, a friend sent me an email asking for my opinion on upcoming digital trends. I copied and pasted my answer into a blog post and my email response morphed into "7 Digital Marketing Trends to Embrace Now."

- People ask me a lot of questions, and those questions have become the number one source of post ideas for my blog. It's not unusual for me to pause in the middle of a class and write down a student's question for later consideration on the blog. If they're curious about a subject, perhaps the readers of my blog would be, too.

- A news broadcast featured the account of a 22-year-old woman who wrote a blog post that prompted a change in bank policy. I thought, "I must know more!" I did a web search on the woman and developed a case study that I've used in my blog, speeches, and a book.

You see, my catalog of new ideas isn't coming from a flash of personal insight or alien intelligence beaming into my head. It's maintained through an awareness of my environment and developing a nose for news.

Anybody can develop this habit. Getting into a content "groove" simply means maintaining this discipline and then scheduling several hours of quiet time each week to reflect on your cache of ideas and turn them into rich content.

As I said at the beginning of this chapter, there's an entire world wide web of help out there to teach you how to become an effective content creator, and I'll leave that in the hands of you and Google. However, there are three fundamental rules of creating effective content that I feel are "can't miss" principles. No matter what type of rich content you choose, keep these three rules in mind.

Rule #1: Add your own story

The world doesn't need another post entitled "Common Twitter mistakes." However, I would read posts with headlines that offer something original, like:

- "Five things I want to destroy on Twitter"

- "The five strangest tweets I've ever seen"

- "How Twitter saved my marriage"

- "The 20 stupidest things you can do on Twitter"

That last one? I actually wrote that post. It was my first "viral" blog post because it was retweeted by Pee-wee Herman, who has 3 million Twitter followers. When he shared it with his audience, it drove so much traffic to my website that it shut down my server. My business temporarily melted from the Pee-wee Heat.

To stand out, you need to be original, and to be original, you must possess the courage to add your own narrative to the mix. There's only one you. You have no competition. **Never publish content that can be created by someone else.**

The ultimate goal of your content is to build an emotional connection between you and your audience. Truly human content leads to awareness, awareness leads to trust, and trust leads to loyalty.

What are some characteristics of human content?

- Vulnerable

- Personal

- Bold

- Unguarded

- Generous

- Confident

A common issue is deciding how much "humanity" is best for your personal brand. Demonstrating honesty and openness doesn't mean spilling your guts. To me, human content builds empathy and connection by offering a glimpse of your personality.

Here's an example: A blogger from Sweden posted a photo of his office setup. He said, "Today, I thought I would show you where I work." This unpretentious piece of content was simple, but it created intimacy by revealing something personal.

On the other end of the scale, there are many who have become known by sharing their lives in the open, like Jenni Prokopy. While working in the construction industry, Jenni started a passion project on the side, a blog called "ChronicBabe" to help other women who live with chronic illness.

At the age of 25, Jenni was diagnosed with fibromyalgia. Soon after came diagnoses of asthma, anxiety, GERD, thyroid disease, and more. She struggled for years, taking test after test and trying an assortment of medications, diets and health programs in an effort to control her symptoms.

Through ChronicBabe, Jenni reveals the travails of her daily life to teach other young women how to live with confidence, have a successful career, and nurture lifelong relationships.

Her personal brand has now become her full-time business. She's known for her transparency and acceptance of imperfection but has struggled at times to find a personal/public balance, especially when she was going through a divorce. Was she revealing too much, or would she become irrelevant if she portrayed a picture of herself that was too curated? Ultimately, she discovered that when she had the courage to be vulnerable, her audience respected her and trusted her even more.

There is undeniable power in being present through your content. Your personal lessons can instruct and inspire. But you don't need to feel guilty or phony because you don't share *everything*. We all edit our public images to some extent, and that's OK. You have a *personal* brand, but you're not a brand like a Snickers bar ready to be plucked from a shelf. They aren't the same thing.

I'm a private person, and I have to push myself to disclose aspects of my life in public. And yet, each time I open up a little, I'm greatly rewarded by reader feedback. I've become more open because my audience wants me to be. Rock star Pete Townshend once said, "I would have enjoyed keeping my private pain out of my work. But I was changed by my audience who said your private pain, which you have unwittingly shown us in your songs, is also ours."

You see, we create content. But content also creates us.

I use transparency in my writing to reinforce that we're all equal in our human condition. We all suffer and stumble through life at times. I also reveal details of my life as indicators of my values. I think it's fair for my audience to know what I stand for. Setting a boundary allows me to create human content in a way that feels honest and comfortable.

Whatever decision you make, maintaining your personal brand shouldn't feel like identity labor or like you're putting on an act. Choose what to share, but don't be a fake. In the process of becoming known, you get to decide what is part of your professional persona and what isn't. You don't have to follow someone else's path or the expectations social media tends to set for us. And your audience – the *right* one, anyway – won't judge you for your choices. They'll cheer you all the way.

Rule #2: Answering and insights

A great way to begin your content journey is to start with answers and end with insights. Let's unpack that idea.

If you're in a niche without much competition, an easy way to begin creating content is to brainstorm every question you can dream of related to your sustainable interest, and then answer them through a blog, video, or podcast. This is an effective way to dominate an uncontested niche and possibly attract search engine attention through "hygiene" content, which I explain in the previous chapter.

Here's a trick to get you going: Go to a website called AnswerThePublic.com. On this site, you enter keywords and it delivers questions people are typing into Google about that topic. Essentially, it's a content idea generator!

Answering customer questions is a solid strategy for beginners, but it's not ideal in every situation, especially in a more crowded content niche. In that situation, you need to focus on *insights* instead of just answers.

For example, I often write on the topic of marketing strategy. I consulted with AnswerThePublic.com and found that a popular topic for me would be "Why Social Media is Important." I Googled this phrase and got 255 million results. That's an incredibly saturated topic. If I were to write a blog post to answer that question, I would only be contributing to the noise!

For me to become known in that information-dense environment, I'd have to do something bold, like offer "hub" content – case studies, opinion pieces, research insights, and strategies you won't find anywhere else.

An advantage of hub content is that it's more likely to keep readers (or viewers) on your site. With hygiene content, after people get an answer to their question, they leave your site and go back to their lives. Hub content is more likely to attract readers who will stay and look around to learn more.

Here are three individuals becoming known by pushing beyond the ordinary question/answer format:

- Mimi Thorisson became a celebrity in the highly competitive world of food blogging by combining astonishing photography, art, and recipes in a blog called Manger (French for "to eat"). Her consistent and beautiful work has led to a television show, book, and speaking appearances.

- On the site IQuantNY, statistician Ben Wellington tells stories of what public data means to citizens of New York. His blog provides fascinating revelations about the city's budget, sewage, parks, and nightlife, among other topics. The popular blog has helped propel his career as an educator and analyst.

- Momastery is a mommy blog about "unleashing the sister warrior." Blogger Glennon Doyle Melton brings her extraordinary heart, humor, and bravery to her storytelling, which she has leveraged into best-selling books and a successful speaking career.

Answering questions is a great place to start, but consider adding bolder and more insightful types of content over time to grow your actionable audience.

Rule #3: Follow the RITE path

Here's a proven method to create consistently good content: Put it to the RITE test.

RITE is my acronym that stands for Relevant, Interesting, Timely, and Entertaining. If you create content that hits at least three out of these four angles, you'll be spinning gold, my friend. Let's take a deeper look.

RELEVANT

What if you have multiple interests, like books, pets, and cars? Can you create content about *everything* you're interested in?

The answer is ... kind of.

You can't confuse people. If you started a video series about woodworking and then did a commentary on French history, your viewers would think, "What's going on here? I came here for the woodworking tips!"

That's not to say you can't bring your hobbies and interests into your content, though. Here's an example of how I did it.

I mentor a young man named Elijah who's an outstanding athlete and very active in sports, so I find myself attending a lot of games. At one basketball game, Elijah's team was pummeling the opponent at halftime by a score of 48-0.

Finally, in the second half, a scrawny little guy on the other team stole a pass, dribbled down the court, and made a beautiful lay-up. But the entire gymnasium gasped in horror because the player had run in the wrong direction and made a basket in the opposing team's hoop. The poor kid scored for the other team!

This made me think, "Just goes to show you. It doesn't matter how well you execute if your strategy is wrong in the first place!" And that became the topic of a blog post. I told this story in my post and used an everyday observation about sports as a teachable moment. I've used inspiration from history, art, travel, literature, and other areas of interest to enliven my blog posts, but the inspiration and stories are all relevant to my core topic.

INTERESTING

Publishing your content isn't a creative writing contest. It's a war for attention. Every single piece of content you produce must be interesting. If you can't do that consistently, you'll lose your audience to competitors who can hold their attention.

How do you stay consistently interesting?

When I create content that's particularly provocative, somebody in the comment section almost always writes, "How did you know this was on my mind?" or, "How did you know we were just talking about this at work?"

I suppose the trick is that I don't just *think* about things that interest me – I *write* about them and start a public discussion. It takes some guts to put yourself out there, especially when a view is incomplete or controversial, but that's the key to remaining interesting, isn't it?

You don't need all the answers to be interesting. You simply have to ask the right *questions*.

TIMELY

One of my biggest advantages is that I don't have a formal editorial calendar. Sounds crazy, but being flexible and tuned in to the world allows me to create content that is "first to market" on breaking news and trending ideas.

Here are opportunities to create content based on changes going on in your environment:

- **Jump on "wow" news:** In every industry, there's someone producing a newsletter that curates the latest news, (If there isn't, go do that!) Read this news every day. If there's a news item that makes you go "wow!" it's probable that others are going "wow," too. Open your laptop at that moment and write a post about the implications of that news from your point of view. Publish that same day and your readers will love you.

- **Comment on a commentary:** Let's say your sustainable interest is firefighting. If an event occurs that affects your industry like a budget cut, a new regulation, or a technological breakthrough, there's news already out there about it. Do a web search to find others commenting on the issue and then 1) summarize their points, 2) provide a link to the original source with attribution, and 3) add your own perspective to the original view.

- **Create a round-up post:** If there's a breakthrough in your area of sustainable interest, ask thought leaders to send you a paragraph, video clip, or soundbite of their views and present a round-up of opinions. You'll create great content with the secondary benefit of quoting industry leaders who may share your post.

ENTERTAINING

Why do you share a piece of content? Because it's entertaining in some way. Maybe the video, podcast, or photo makes you laugh, inspires you, or amazes you.

Thinking in terms of entertainment may create a point of differentiation for you and your content. Most people aren't putting their content through the entertainment filter ... they're just reporting. Could you stand out from the crowd and become known because of your entertaining style? Entertainment is the final factor in the RITE formula, but it's perhaps the most important aspect of content creation today.

Before I publish any piece of content, I think about how I can make it more Relevant, Interesting, Timely, and Entertaining, and I know this is a concept that will work for you, too.

I hope I've helped you put your fears in a proper place and that you'll commit to creating content that will be rewarding and fun for you and your audience.

Wait ... you DO have an audience, don't you? No? Well, let's go find one.

CHAPTER 7

Step Four: Creating an Actionable Audience

"My interaction with the audience is something that makes me come alive. It's a feeling like no other. The energy of the crowd fuels something new inside." – Alicia Keys, singer

If content is your fuel, the audience is your fire.

Nothing makes the process of becoming known more gratifying than the moment you realize somebody out there is listening. In fact, the value of your content is zero unless somebody views it. So, the final step in your process to become known is finding your fans.

When it comes to building an audience, Elsie Larson, one of the sisters behind the do-it-yourself website "A Beautiful Mess," reflects a unifying sentiment of everyone I interviewed for this book.[1]

"I built a readership over the course of many years," Elsie said. "I focused on quality posts that take a lot of time to write and develop, being consistent (I've been posting almost every day for several years), and being myself. The blog evolves as

I evolve; it's slow and steady. Nothing happened overnight. I have never paid a penny to advertise 'A Beautiful Mess;' I just kept doing my best and a readership developed over the years. It's the product of hard work, constant evaluation, and lots of love."

Musician Mike Masse has built an enormous audience for his YouTube covers of classic rock songs ... to the point where he's quit his "day job" to make covers his living. He said, "The key to building an audience is 1. Be good, and 2. Don't be bad! You don't have to be a master of your craft, but just begin, and work on continuous improvement. Find people in your area of interest who know more about it than you do, and become a sponge. And, in turn, be willing to share what you know with others.

"It's not about quality versus quantity," Mike said. "You need both. The more you put out there, the more ways there are for people to find you. Overwhelm the world with evidence of your irrefutable awesomeness. That's how you build an audience."

Lorraine Loots, the miniatures artist from South Africa introduced in Chapter 2, said: "Forget about playing some game to gain followers on social media, and instead focus your time on creating good quality content, and putting it out there consistently."

These themes should be familiar to you by now. Quality. Consistency. A unique and authentic "place." Hard work.

Still, if you're starting from scratch, you probably have some audience anxiety. What if you build it and nobody comes? In this chapter, I'll cover some of the most popular methods to attract people to your content (and keep them there), including:

- **Passive connection** and building an audience through the help of SEO, social media, paid promotion, and other bloggers.

- **Active connection** through engagement, networking, and influencers.

I'll provide specific tips you can use today for each of these ideas, and I'll wrap up the chapter with a key objective: Developing the all-important *alpha audience*.

But first, I need to bust two myths about audience-building. Let's start with myth number one: The idea that you need a million fans to be successful.

Perhaps you need just five ...

The big enough niche

Dr. Alice Ackerman is the chairman of a pediatrics department at a Virginia hospital, and her story illustrates an essential lesson about becoming known and building the right audience.

Several years ago, Dr. Ackerman started reading my blog and soon believed that becoming known through the web would be a way for her to teach people about the importance of childhood inoculations. In her region, there was misinformation about vaccinating children, and her mission was to dispel these myths and improve the inoculation rate.

It took some political maneuvering, but she convinced her medical center to allow her to start a blog. That turned out to be the easy part. Finding an audience for her posts was another matter.

Month by month, Dr. Ackerman created helpful content to educate her community on the importance of vaccinating children. But she wondered if she was making an impact. For more than a year, her posts limped along, averaging fewer than five readers a day.

And then something magical occurred.

Dr. Ackerman received a message from a woman who inoculated her children based on what she had read on the blog. "I never knew that information existed," the woman wrote. And she pledged to spread the word until every child in her neighborhood was inoculated, too.

"Yes, I only had five readers a day on my blog," Dr. Ackerman said, "but they were the right five readers. I was known to the right people and I made a difference."

This case study illustrates – in a beautiful way – how becoming known differs from being famous. Dr. Ackerman didn't need an audience of millions or even hundreds. She's never going to be on the red carpet or interviewed by the BBC – and she doesn't need to be. For her to achieve her goal, just one connection can make a difference.

Let's reflect on the estimated primary audience of some of the people you've met in the pages of this book so far:

- Antonio Centeno, video fashion tips: 750,000 YouTube subscribers

- Isadora Becker, recipes for food featured in movies: 180,000 subscribers

- Tom Fishburne, business cartoonist: Tens of thousands of newsletter subscribers

- Suzy Trotta, Knoxville realtor: About 2,000 Twitter followers, mostly in her city

- Lindsey Kirchoff, college student seeking a job: About 500 LinkedIn connections

- Shawn Van Dyke, construction consultant: Dozens of business owners in his private Facebook Group

- Dr. Alice Ackerman, pediatrician: Fewer than 25 blog subscribers

These people are successful in their unique ways and are known in their respective fields, but the size and location of the audiences they need to succeed varies wildly. The lesson here is that there's no universal answer to the question, "How big does my audience need to be?" It depends on who you need to connect with and what you want to achieve.

Life is a long path, and you meet a lot of different people along the way. Maybe all you need is one follower if it's a person who will change the course of your life.

Let's move on to myth number two: Audience equals power.

Audience does not equal activation

Your growing social media connections are merely weak relational links. A "like" represents little more than a handshake. Just because someone has followed you on YouTube or Twitter doesn't mean they'll buy something from you, hire you, or donate to your charity. It simply means the door has been cracked opened. It's raw potential.

This is one of the most misunderstood concepts on the web. Most people think if you have a million Twitter followers, you should be able to get them to do something. "Just think! Even if 1 percent of my Twitter followers buy my book, I'll be a best-selling author."

But it doesn't work that way. Don't believe me? Let me prove it.

Alyssa Milano, a popular American television and movie actress, sent out an unusual tweet to her 3 million followers: a link to the Amazon page of a book called *Connected: The Surprising Power of Our Social Networks and How They Shape Our Lives* by Nicholas Christakis and James Fowler.

An author's dream come true! This had the makings of a viral success story. A book recommendation from a heavily followed Twitter account should lead to a huge spike in sales, right? Amplification, after all, comes from size: The more followers a person has, the more people who will see a message and who will, potentially, retweet it – and, thus, the more people who will probably act on it.

So how many books were sold in the wake of that tweet to 3 million followers?

None.

Literally, not one. In fact, in the days and weeks following Alyssa's tweet, the book's sales declined. The actress's massive audience hadn't been a force for anything. "At least with respect to the influence of behavior," author Christakis noted, "these Twitter links are weak."

Social networks are effective at increasing participation by lessening the level of motivation that participation requires. It takes no effort to click a "like" button, for example. But it takes more investment to act on a person's influence and buy a book, show up at a political rally, or contribute to a charity.

And so, we bust one of the internet's gigantic myths. Audience size does not equal power. There are no shortcuts. To build an actionable audience, you need to establish a legitimate emotional connection with people over time. Let's discover how to do that.

Passive audience activation

Here's the reason the Alyssa Milano tweet fell as flat as a Kansas cornfield: While her adoring fans are eager to sneak a glimpse of her glamorous life or next television project, there was no emotional connection between them and the academic book she promoted. You would see the same (lack of) impact if a famous Formula One driver tweeted, "Hey everyone, sign up for this online cooking class!" It's not a very convincing endorsement.

The key to assembling an audience that can be *activated* is to patiently build a meaningful and relevant emotional connection with them. This can occur two ways: passively or actively.

A passive emotional connection occurs when people come to know you through your content alone, typically over a long period of time. As people begin to see and enjoy your work, they progress through four phases of an emotional journey:

- **Awareness:** They discover your content and know you exist. Perhaps 98 percent of the people who find you will move on, but a few will stick around to move to the next phase. That's why it's important to constantly build awareness and attract potential new fans.

- **Engagement:** The new connections want to see more. They may click on a link, explore your website, comment on your blog, and even share your content with friends. It's starting to become a two-way connection. They are learning about you and liking what they see.

- **Stable connection:** New fans opt-in. They subscribe to your newsletter or follow you on Facebook, LinkedIn, or another channel. Your content is adding enough value to their lives that they want to follow your work regularly. For the first time, you may know a fan exists because they're subscribing to you. A subscription means, "I trust you and I want to see more."

- **Loyalty:** Your fan not only follows you but encourages

others to follow you, too. This is the elite group that's most likely to be activated. They'll spread your ideas, donate to your charity, or hire you to speak at an event. Your ideas and your content are becoming a part of the fabric of their lives. They can't get enough of you.

Here's an example of how this passive bond works. I received an email that went something like this: "Mr. Schaefer, I've read your blog for three years now and have also read your books and distributed them to others in my company. We feel that you have the right expertise to help us develop our marketing strategy. Can we discuss that possibility?"

The email came from a vice president of one of the most recognized retail brands on the planet. I had never heard of this fan before ... we had no previous interaction that I could recall. But through my content alone he felt like he knew me and trusted me enough to reach out and ultimately hire me. This passive emotional connection resulted in the biggest consulting contract of my career.

Tom Fishburne, The Marketoonist, has a similar approach to building a meaningful audience through passive connection to his content.

"I started building my audience very simply, by emailing a cartoon to 35 coworkers at General Mills in 2000," he said. "I just asked if anyone would like to see my weekly cartoon about marketing. That was it. That's the only push I've ever done! From there, it was purely about trying to create better and better cartoons. By focusing on the quality of the cartoons and paying attention to how my audience responded to them, the audience largely took care of itself."

You live in the most amazing time. Like Tom, if you do supremely good work, you can earn an audience that builds itself. At no other time in history have we had an opportunity like that without the benefit of a book contract, a political appointment, or a large bank account. You can earn an audience by being you, at your best.

The number of people who move all the way from awareness to loyalty will be small. That's why it's important to constantly seek exposure to fill the pipeline. Here are four essential techniques to do that:

SEARCH ENGINE OPTIMIZATION

Search engine optimization (SEO) is a practice to assure that your content is friendly to sites like Google and the algorithms they use to deliver search results. Optimizing your content for search engines doesn't have to be complicated, and it's critically important to help people find your work. There's an incredible amount of information about SEO available on the web (as well as people trying to sell you their services), so don't feel like you have to learn it all at once. Luckily, sites like WordPress (the leading blogging platform), Slideshare, Pinterest, and YouTube have built-in SEO features that allow you to easily add tags and descriptive headlines that help Google find you. There are also free plug-ins like Yoast to help optimize your blog.

Google rewards sites that have fresh, frequent, and popular content, and that's something you can build up over time by consistently posting about your sustainable interest. If you're just starting out, it's smart to learn a little about basic SEO practices. I recommend that you search for something like "how do I optimize my blog/video/podcast" to learn a few best practices. Building basic SEO into your content from the beginning can save you work later.

As you progress with your activities, you may want to dive more deeply into the subject and perhaps get professional assistance, but remember that the very best thing you can do for SEO is to create helpful, relevant, and timely content. Don't obsess about SEO – just get going and get a little better at it over time.

SOCIAL MEDIA

Sites like Facebook, Pinterest, and Instagram are revolutionary opportunities for establishing a personal brand, and they're vitally important channels for distributing your content.

Every social media site has pros and cons (and the rules keep changing!). There's no single strategy that fits every person, but if I had to pick one distribution channel for your content, it would be Twitter. That may be surprising since Twitter isn't the biggest or most popular network, but it has hundreds of millions of active users and offers distinct advantages over other channels:

- Twitter allows you to connect to anyone (including influencers) and engage with them, even if they don't follow you back.

- Twitter profiles are always public, and there are many free, independent applications to help you find relevant new audience members.

- There's a ton of engagement on Twitter. By comparison, LinkedIn is a great place to find connections, but there isn't a lot of chit-chat going on there.

- Twitter doesn't control your content flow. Facebook severely edits your newsfeed because there's so much content available. Depending on your topic and audience, you may have almost no chance of reaching people on Facebook without paying for an advertising boost. All content on Twitter is delivered equally and free of charge.

If people like you on Twitter, they'll probably like your content too. Feel free to promote a new post or video to your new

Twitter friends. Showing them your original ideas will certainly help strengthen your brand.

Rand Fishkin, the SEO software entrepreneur I introduced in Chapter 6, built an audience for his blog and video content almost entirely on Twitter. "When Twitter emerged, it took off in the business world and I've continued to engage a lot on that platform," he said. "That external participation helped build our community and awareness for my content. Today we connect with our audience in a lot of ways including forums, a conference, and event sponsorships. But the initial success I had was almost entirely organic, through social media."

Here are five ways to build your audience through Twitter-related tactics:

1. **Mine Twitter Lists.** Once you're on Twitter for a while, you'll notice that people place you on public lists. Twitter Lists are a superb way to find relevant people to follow. Lists are generally categorized by a special interest or geographic location. For example, I might be on lists for "marketing experts" or "business educators." Once you find a relevant person to follow, dig into their Lists and you're likely to find a goldmine of similar people to follow.

2. **Search for related hashtags.** Do a search on Twitter by your topical interests and follow those who pop up in the results. For example, if you're in construction, try searching by #construction, #building, #architecture, or #remodeling.

3. **Join Twitter Chats.** Twitter Chats are regularly scheduled online meetings based on special interests. There are chats available for almost any topic you can think of. Do a web search for "Twitter Chats" and you'll find

a list of schedules. When you attend a chat, you'll discover many new connections with common interests you can follow.

4. **Keep up with live tweeting.** At many industry events, attendees tweet about their experiences as a generous way to share information with those who can't attend. At large events, there may be thousands of people around the world following an event hashtag. For example, let's say your sustainable interest has something to do with dogs. Each February, you'll find people tweeting about the #WestminsterDogShow. Many could be high-potential followers for you.

5. **Use Advanced Search.** Twitter has an extremely useful advanced search function – the only problem is finding it since it's not on the main Twitter site. To discover it, do a search for "Twitter advanced search." The menu-driven application can help you find people to follow by keyword, location, and other useful parameters.

There's no one-size-fits-all approach to building an audience through social media. Twitter will work for many, but it's also very limited in some ways and may exclude key audiences (the platform isn't popular in some countries, for example).

Don't feel pressured to extend your social media presence beyond your comfort level. A quality presence on a couple of platforms will serve you better than a weak existence on many. So experiment a little. As time goes on, you'll discover which platforms work best for you – where you get the most followers, where you find it most enjoyable to share, and what best supports traffic to your content.

ADVERTISING AND PROMOTION

In a noisy world, many people utilize some form of paid advertising or promotion to attract attention to their content. Here's a rundown of a few of the most popular techniques from Chad Pollitt, cofounder of the Relevance Agency and an expert on paid content promotion:

Paid social media: This is the technique that may be most familiar to you. Facebook, Twitter, and LinkedIn all provide a variety of flexible, creative, and highly targeted advertising solutions. A best practice is to use a form of paid social media to further boost your best-performing content (not your worst). You can have a significant impact for as little as $50 a week. Another idea is to set up your ads to target the journalists, influencers, and bloggers who might be most interested in your content. If your boosted content gets shared by others, there's no additional cost.

Sponsored content: Have you ever seen a special advertising section in an in-flight magazine? That's a form of sponsored content, and there are options that allow anyone to employ this technique. It's possible to pay to post one of your articles on many blogs, trade publications, and even traditional media outlets like *Forbes*. As more publishers seek new monetization options, sponsored content is becoming a popular (and perhaps overused) option. The content must always be clearly marked as "sponsored."

Native advertising: This is sort of a sneaky way to embed mentions of your brand in the editorial portion of news articles. The content is displayed within the normal reading stream of the website, so it looks like it's supposed to be there as opposed to banner ads that are gaudy and obnoxious. Native advertising is becoming an extremely popular technique as well as a controversial one because it blurs the line between journalism and advertising.

Recommendation widgets: These are the ad units you typically see at the bottom of an article that "recommend" other articles to read. As a content creator, you can pay to have your content placed on thousands of different websites. What makes this type of advertising so appealing is the scale it provides at a relatively low cost.

RELATED BLOGGERS

You can make real-life friends through blogging, and the encouragement and advice from fellow bloggers is easily worth more than any new traffic or growth you might achieve. You can foster new friendships by commenting, emailing, and of course linking and highlighting other blogs that you love in your own content.

Bloggers you enjoy might return the favors (linking back, commenting, etc.), and you can send a few readers each other's way. Take the slow approach by building an honest and friendly rapport instead of blasting everyone with requests to share your links.

There are a number of online clubs where bloggers can help and support each other. These include independent blogger sites, LinkedIn Groups, and Facebook Groups. There are also many specialty blogger conferences that are great for networking.

Another way to connect with fellow bloggers is guest posts. Contributing a guest post to a popular industry site can provide an immediate boost for your own work. If you befriend a fellow blogger and offer them an extraordinary content contribution, it's a win-win for everyone.

You can grow your following quickly by using these tools and techniques, but most people who want to be known don't simply publish content and wait for something to happen. They push things along in a more active way. There are three different strategies for active audience building: engagement, networking, and influencers. Let's look at each of these concepts more closely.

Audience activation: Engagement

The easiest way to build an emotional connection with your audience is to acknowledge them and let them know you care.

When I was starting out as a blogger, I sent a tweet to personally thank every person who retweeted me. I mailed handwritten thank you notes to industry leaders who mentioned me in a post. I responded to every reader comment on my blog posts. I've even called people out of the blue when they've said something nice about me on the web.

One of the most effective forms of engagement I've seen involved homemade chocolate chip cookies. A young woman commented on one of my blog posts and told me she was struggling with a question. Rather than answer her in a reply comment, I thought it would be more effective to call her and help her through the complex issue. This was my way of reaching out and building loyalty, and it worked ... but there was a twist.

Through our phone discussion, I learned we had similar interests and marketing viewpoints. I also admired the work she was doing on her website. I suggested to her that there could be ways we could work together in the future.

A few days after our call, I received a package in the mail with homemade chocolate chip cookies as a "thank you" for my help. I was so moved by this thoughtful gesture that I provided her with a few small design jobs, and then bigger jobs, and oh yes ... Sarah Mason is the person who designed the interior and cover of this book! That's the mighty, mighty power of the cookie.

When it comes to building an audience through engagement, Ana Silva O'Reilly is a role model. The Portugal native founded a wildly successful luxury travel blog called Mrs. O Around the World and built a passionate audience by engaging with her readers in a consistent and friendly way.

"After I launched my travel blog, people started asking me questions," Ana said. "Where should I stay? Where should I eat? What should I see? And I would respond to every inquiry, one by one, no matter how long it took. And I still do! That's one of the best things about my blog. I love that like-minded people take the time to listen to what I have to say, and it has created not just fans, but many wonderful friendships.

"I built my audience through tireless engagement," she said. "My greatest reward is when somebody tells me they would have never found some great hotel or restaurant without me. I love helping people in any way I can."

"There's no shortcut," Ana said. "You build loyal readers one person, one connection at a time. Becoming popular is difficult to scale. That's one of the reasons why I don't want the blog to get much bigger than it is. I feel I would lose that connection that makes me stand out."

Brands have noticed Ana and her passionate community and approached her about opportunities to consult and help them create mutually-beneficial content. Her blog, which started as a college class project, has evolved into a rewarding and lucrative career.

Engagement is the glue that connects you to your fans and drives them to that "inner circle." Here are five tips to rouse engagement with your audience:

1. End your blog post or video with a question that encourages a response, like "Those are my views. What do you think? What did I miss?"

2. If there are specific people you want to target for your audience, like a prospective employer, a possible donor, or somebody who has similar interests as you, go to where they are on the web and look for opportunities to engage. Comment on a LinkedIn post, congratulate them

on a professional accomplishment, or mention them in a tweet or post.

3. When you begin to identify specific members of your audience, include them on a Twitter List to make it easy to monitor their activities and find opportunities to comment and engage with them.

4. Crowdsource answers. Are you experiencing a difficult problem? Why not ask your audience to help you and then feature their answers in your content?

5. Be vulnerable. Every now and then, expose something new about yourself. Demonstrating personal courage through your writing almost always elicits an outpouring of engagement and support.

Engagement is also important because it represents a measure that you're heading in the right direction. In the next chapter, I'll suggest how engagement can be an essential leading indicator of future success.

Audience activation: Networking

When marketing technology specialist Ian Cleary goes to a conference, he doesn't attend any of the scheduled sessions. He stands in the hallways … and waits.

"I can usually buy a virtual pass and hear the sessions later at home," he said. "But I don't want to miss an opportunity to meet people in the corridors. That's where most things happen at conferences!"

In fact, this is how Ian met me. I was walking down a hallway at a conference when he literally chased me down, exclaiming, "Mark Schaefer! You're one of my favorite bloggers and I wanted to meet you!"

I'll never forget that moment because it led to so many rewarding personal and professional benefits. Although I was somewhat aware of Ian from his work on social media, it wasn't until we met in real life that we turned a weak relational link into a friendship and partnership that has lasted for years.

During our first meeting at the conference, I mentioned to Ian that I was planning a trip to Dublin, his hometown. He invited me out to dinner during my visit and asked me if I wouldn't mind meeting a few of his friends for a drink while I was there. I agreed.

When I arrived at the Dublin pub at the scheduled time, the bar was desolate. I waited a few minutes and then asked the bartender if I was in the right place. "Oh, they're in the back room," the bartender said. When I walked through the door, I was shocked to find 75 people there, waiting to greet me. I had just entered the Ian Cleary Networking Zone!

At that one pub event, I met people who:

- Invited me to present a paid workshop at a Dublin college

- Asked me to speak at a European Union agency

- Involved me in a global charity to teach computer coding to young children

Ian and I have continued to work together over the years. I was responsible for scheduling his first speaking gig, and he has contributed several posts to my blog. He helped with material for my book *The Content Code,* and we've taught a college course together.

Not bad for one hallway meeting!

Ian is a master at building deep relationships by seeking every opportunity to transform a weak social media connection into a strong one through some personal touchpoint. That's when the magic begins.

Here are five tips to transform your weak relational links into strong ones through networking:

1. Keep a list of your most active audience members, by city. When you visit a city for pleasure or business, pull out your list and invite your audience members for coffee.

2. Make time each month for a Skype call to get to know at least one person from your audience.

3. Interview somebody from your audience for your blog, podcast, or video. Use that interaction as an excuse to build a closer relationship.

4. Start a chain reaction of reciprocity by going out of your way to send a card or personal note to those who are sharing your content and supporting you.

5. Make yourself available. When I'm on a long car ride, I tweet out that I'm available for a phone call to keep me company along the way. If someone responds, I send a private message with my phone number. This has created some of the most amazing friendships!

Audience activation: Influence

As you've seen in the case studies throughout this book, people become known by finding their place and space and then creating consistent content over a period of time. But what if you don't have that time? What if you have to be known NOW? That's when it's time to connect with influencers.

One of the most charming examples of finding an unsaturated space and using influencers to become known comes from Aaron Lee of Malaysia.

Aaron is no stranger to branding. He had already established himself as a social media marketing star in Asia. But his options in Malaysia were limited, and when he found himself out of work, he decided to carve out a sustainable interest in fashion ... by leveraging his height. Or more accurately, his lack of it.

"I love fashion and I like to look sharp, but realistically, I knew that I was unlikely to succeed in the fashion blogging world," he said. "I had no experience in fashion and I live in a historic city on a tropical peninsula in Malaysia. Not exactly Paris or New York!"

But when Aaron did some research on fashion topics, he found there was almost no competition when it came to advice for short men. And at 5 feet 4 inches tall, Aaron was a natural subject matter expert.

"I knew I couldn't just write about fashion," he said. "I could never make a name for myself in that crowded space. I needed my own angle, and it seemed like I could take advantage of my height."

Aaron used his connections with influencers to help drive his brand quickly. "There are many benefits to working with influencers," he said. "But probably the greatest one is rapid exposure. These influencers may have tens of thousands of followers. It's all about figuring out what you can do for them ... not the other way around.

"For example, I noticed a fashion page with more than 200,000 followers on Instagram. They share high-quality pictures of fashionable people who post in other places on Instagram. I offered to provide them exclusive, high-quality images of myself that would look great on their account. They loved the idea and they've posted more than 20 of my photos.

I've built my audience by thousands of new followers just from that exposure.

"For other influencers, I've written guest posts, or even sent them little handcrafted gifts as a way to be thoughtful. It's all about figuring out what they want and how I can help them.

"No matter what topic you want to be known for, you should be proactive with industry leaders," Aaron said. "You need to mingle with other influencers who can help you along the way. The best approach is to leave your digital footprint everywhere. Do this by liking other people's photos, commenting on blog posts, helping others out, retweeting, creating guest content on leading blogs, and participating in Twitter chats, to name a few ideas."

Even in a saturated segment, people are open to original ideas and new authorities to follow. Having your content presented to them by a trusted influencer could be just what it takes to attract high-potential new followers.

How do you find influencers who can make a difference to you? Here are five tips to find the people who are having an impact in your field:

1. Use BuzzSumo's free influencer search tool. You can use keywords and find Twitter handles of accounts sharing similar keyword-related content. Filters let you sort results by reach, authority, influence, and engagement.

2. Try Followerwonk, a free app on Rand Fishkin's Moz site. This tool lets you search Twitter users based on keywords in their bios and sort results based on their number of followers and social authority.

3. Twellow is a very useful site that can help you build your audience in several ways. It allows you to search influencers by industry and breaks down results based on lo-

cation, subject matter, and profession. Another way to find possible influencers by location is to Google it. For example, searching for "mommy bloggers in Pittsburgh" would return lists of top bloggers in the area.

4. Check out industry-related conferences and scan the speaker list. These are likely to be well-known and influential leaders in your field.

5. Hashtag research can help you identify influencers with similar interests. Search for a topical hashtag (like #organicfood, #librarian, or #electricalengineer, for example) on Google, Twitter, and Instagram to find others interested in a topic. Dig a little deeper to look at how many followers they have, the engagement they get on their posts, and what kind of content they publish.

Once you've created a list of influencers, it's time to start finding ways to connect with them. We learned some important lessons from Aaron Lee and Shawn Van Dyke, the construction business owner introduced in Chapter 5. Don't "pitch" influencers. Befriend them.

Shawn gave away his consulting services to a powerful industry authority, and that propelled him to rapid success. Aaron is a master of finding small gifts that show he's paying attention to the leaders he admires.

Help influencers before you have any expectation of them helping you. Subscribe to their blog or video channel, follow them on Twitter, like them on Facebook. Look for opportunities to engage through a blog comment, a congratulatory message on LinkedIn, or a tweet. Nothing says "I love you" more than a retweet now and then.

Mention influencers in your own blogs and content. Highlight great work they've done. When you link to their work in your own content, there's a good chance they'll get a notification (called a "ping") and perhaps notice that you did it.

These little touchpoints add to your bank of social capital. Don't try to make a withdrawal from that bank (like asking for a favor) until you've made some contributions of your own.

The Alpha Audience

I started this chapter by noting that the value of your content is zero unless somebody views it. In essence, people viewing and sharing your content drives the economics of everything you do, so I can't end this chapter without mentioning the most special segment of all, your Alpha Audience.

I first introduced this concept in my book *The Content Code. Alpha Audience* refers to an elite circle of people – probably less than 2 percent of your entire social media following – who are responsible for sharing your content the most.

Research points to the amazing benefits provided by this special tribe:

- The act of sharing content creates advocacy. When people share your content, in a virtual way they're saying, "I believe in this, and you should too."

- Sharing content promotes understanding. According to a study by *The New York Times*, 85 percent of the people who share content say they better understand the person or organization who created it. The simple reason is that they're probably not going to share content unless they trust you.

- According to the Boston Consulting Group, the recommendations of the Alpha Audience account for eight times their own purchases.

Do you know who shares your content the most? Do you know your Alpha Audience ... by name? If you spend any time at all nurturing an emotional connection with your followers, it should be with these special people.

At this point in the book we've covered the four basic steps to become known. Way to go! From this chapter, you should be adding the following to your plan:

- Ideas to continuously and mindfully build the size of your relevant audience

- Opportunities to deepen the relationships with your audience through engagement, networking, and selectively connecting with trusted influencers

- An awareness of the importance of the Alpha Audience, the people who become advocates when they share your content consistently

I'm convinced the plan I've covered is repeatable and achievable. If you follow this path with consistency and energy, you'll be on your way.

But maybe you're ready for a little more. Do you really want to blow it up and achieve massive reach with your personal brand? Are you ready to become known on an entirely new level?

Of course you are. In that case, read on. You've reached the bonus level.

CHAPTER 8

Taking Your Brand to the Next Level

"If you want to know yourself, start by writing a book."
– Shereen El Feki, journalist and activist

Allow me to twist your mind for a moment. For many of the people we've met in these pages, becoming known has led to a successful career writing books and giving speeches. But writing books and giving speeches can also help you become known in the first place.

So, which comes first?

Following the four-step path of this book – developing a place, a space, your content, and an audience – will certainly put you on a track to become known. That might be all you'll need to do to achieve your goals. However, if you want to super-charge your presence, you should consider advanced strategies like writing a book or developing a speaking career.

For many, the thrill of writing a book or taking the stage may be the goal of becoming known. And these activities can also build your authority and your audience at any stage of the journey.

These activities represent bold moves that may be *way* out of your comfort zone. But consider ... at the beginning of the journey to become known, is writing a book or speaking on a stage in *anybody's* comfort zone? Probably not, and yet people find a way to overcome the fear and blast ahead.

In this chapter, I'll explore the benefits and challenges of these activities. If writing a book or speaking seem improbable for you at this stage in your life, feel free to skip this chapter. It's just something I want you to consider, for now or the future.

The Top Five Reasons to Write a Book

1. **Credibility**: Being known as an author of a book awards you a certain permanent bump in status. As long as you live, you'll be known as the author of your book. Writing a book is an exceptional, high-status accomplishment. In a world of so much free and easy media, a book is still rare.

2. **High visibility**: Whenever a news reporter wants a comment for a story, who do they go to? The expert. And how do they know someone is an expert? Because they wrote the book.

3. **Forging expertise**: The process of writing this book – from the germ of an idea to a product I can hold in my hand – took two years of studying, researching, interviewing, and writing. I was not an expert at becoming known when I started the book. I am now. Writing this book awarded me the equivalent of a master's degree in personal branding! My new expertise can open new doors because I did this hard work.

4. **Helping people find you**: The number one search engine

is Google. Number two is YouTube. Can you guess number three? Amazon.

5. **New income source:** But not from the book. I'll tell you why in a moment.

The Top Five Reasons NOT to Write a Book

1. You may spend months of time away from your family and activities that you love.

2. You'll make very little money directly from this incredible time investment.

3. It's one of the most difficult tasks you'll ever complete.

4. Your book may not be very good, and bad reviews are soul-crushing.

5. It's incredibly difficult to come up with an idea that you can sustain for 50,000 words or more.

Writing a book is a big decision – and a very personal one. Taken altogether, I'm convinced the benefits of writing a book outweigh the negatives, and if you have the ability and the will to do it, you should dive in. But first let's say hello to the elephant in the room: money.

Since I'm in the writing business, I have a lot of friends who write books, too. They're young, they're eager, and they're convinced their first book will change their financial fortunes. It doesn't. Ever.

Not "maybe."

Not "you never know."

Never.

The average number of books sold by nominees for the National Book Award in America is 3,000 copies. That's practically nothing ... and these are the books that people consider the best of the best!

In a typical year, there are about 300,000 new books published in America. Nielsen BookScan, the company that measures all book sales, reports that about 200 books per year sell 100,000 copies, and they're almost all novels by established, famous writers.

I know this flies in the face of the whole "follow your dream" thing, but those are the facts, folks. Once you get through your list of family and friends, it's excruciatingly hard to sell a first book. There are many good reasons to write a book, but only if you adopt the proper mindset and realize that direct book sales will *not* be one of those reasons.

Now that I've told you that you won't make money from books, here are a few ways you can make money from books (other than sales!):

- **Consulting services:** Expertise established through a book can be leveraged through consulting assignments. For example, one benefit of this book could be that individuals and organizations hire me to help them become known.

- **Speaking:** Turning core ideas from your book into a speech is a natural opportunity. An example of this is Dorie Clark. She transformed herself from out-of-work journalist to well-paid speaker before organizations such as the World Bank and Harvard University. She attributes most of her success to her two books.

- **Selling a product:** In Chapter 2 we met Joe Wicks, the successful fitness trainer from the U.K. He wrote a book on nutrition, but what he's really selling is a diet plan.

- **Create a mastermind group:** As you build an audience, they may be eager to learn more from you and get a firsthand dose of your expertise. A popular format is the "mastermind" group that allows people to meet with you in a virtual forum, generally to present original content and answer questions. These groups vary widely from a few dollars a month to tens of thousands of dollars to access top experts.

- **Client access:** Having the weighty authority of a book can help open doors for direct customer acquisition.

So yes, you *can* make money from a book, in these ways and more, but for most people the big payoff will simply be an astonishing boost in awareness, the true currency of becoming known! In fact, other than the consistent production of a blog, podcast, or video series, there's probably no single project that can help you grow your personal authority more than writing a book.

How to write a book (and finish the job)

There are countless resources on the web to teach you how to write a book. That sort of tutorial is far beyond the scope of this book. However, I want to provide an accurate and high-level view of what's involved as well as an inside view of my process that might help you.

THE MAIN IDEA

The most challenging part of writing a book is coming up with an idea that is singular and exciting. This is my sixth book. I never had a plan to write six books, or any books for that matter, but when I come across a problem that's just so big that I can't figure it out without a lot of work, an idea begins to take shape.

My assumption is that you're not writing a work of fiction. You want to write something that will help you become known in your career field. How do you get that big idea? Here are a few prompts:

- Research: Do you have access to revelations from original research? This has been the starting point for many great business books, for example.

- Expertise: Do you possess extraordinary insight because you're the best in your field?

- Personal: Do you have a story of transformation that can inspire?

- Vision: Do you have an image of the future that is unique and compelling?

- Solution to a problem: Can you guide people through a complicated process (like I'm doing in this book), or can you teach them to do something?

Whatever topic you choose, you must *love* it. You must be fixated by it, in fact, because you're going to be spending a lot of time with it. When I wrote *The Content Code,* every marketer in my field was facing a problem: How do we get our messages heard in an increasingly noisy world? As a marketing strategist, *I had to figure this out.* I became obsessed with finding the answer. It was extremely hard work and required a big sacrifice of time and energy, but I had an overwhelming feeling of purpose, as I do with this book.

THE OUTLINE

Once I have a concept, I create an outline of what I believe the book's chapters will be. I use an inexpensive application called Evernote to create a file folder for each chapter. Throughout the year, as I discover articles, collect research, or interview prospects for the book, I make myself a little note about it in the appropriate electronic file. This way, when it's time to write, I have most of the resources I need right at my fingertips.

The idea is to prepare as much as you can before the writing commences. Once you begin to write, you won't want to be distracted by research or interviews – you'll need to stay in the zone and focus.

Don't be afraid to adjust the outline as you learn more about the topic. In fact, don't be afraid to change the whole book. Stay open to new ideas and new truths. Sticking to preconceived notions of the truth can be dangerous for a writer. Let the research write the book.

THE WRITING BEGINS

An average-sized book contains about 60,000 words. I find it impossible to tell a story that long when I'm working in little portions of time. If you keep stopping and starting, you'll waste effort just figuring out where you are in the process, and the book will take twice as long to write.

For an intense process like writing a book, I need to block out big chunks of time. Maybe weeks of time. I realize that's hard for most people to do, especially if you have a job, kids to raise, and a spouse to love. For me, the only time I can write is over the holiday season when my business trips and college classes slow down.

Another trick is to create a speech first about your book topic. If you record a standard 45-minute speech and have it transcribed, you'll have about 30,000 words – that's half a book!

TESTING IDEAS

Before I commit a radical new idea to the permanent fixture of a book, I test it through a blog post. For example, in my last book, I proposed a controversial idea about the relationship between content and search engine optimization. I wrote a blog post about the concept to test the waters, and everybody seemed to think it made sense, so I had complete confidence that the idea should be in the book. In essence, I used my blog as a research center.

In one example, I floated an idea on a blog post and some of the reader comments were so extraordinary that I included them in the book. I also tested ideas for this book with a trusted group of friends in a private Facebook Group. Their feedback is embedded in every chapter.

REWRITING AND EDITING

There's no such thing as good writing, only good rewriting. Writing the first draft of a book is like creating a monumental sculpture with a chainsaw – it's all there, and you can kind of tell what it is, but you need to do a lot of grinding and polishing to create a finished product!

Author Shannon Hale once said, "I'm writing a first draft and reminding myself that I'm simply shoveling sand into a box so I can build castles later."

There are several specialized software programs for writers, but Microsoft Word is perfectly fine for just about any book you could write. In fact, this is the format most traditional publishers prefer.

If you don't have a book contract and a publisher to help you, you'll have to hire an editor. This is an indispensable step, even if you're an experienced writer. Every author needs a set of professional eyes to take a final look at every pronoun and punctuation mark.

HOW TO PUBLISH

I've published six books, three through a publisher and three on my own. In my view, there are few, if any, downsides to self-publishing a book today. The traditional publishing industry is in a state of implosion, and self-publishing is becoming easier all the time. Let's break this down into the four main advantages that are supposed to be provided by a mainstream publisher:

- **An advance:** The typical advance for an unknown author is around $10,000. With the declining state of the industry, publishers have tried to reduce or even eliminate that amount. If you're lucky enough to get an advance these days, you must pay it back from your book sales, as the name "advance" implies. Obviously you don't get an advance if you self-publish, but some of my books have had sponsors who contributed more money than I would have received with an advance (and I don't have to pay it back). I can then put that money into …

- **Marketing:** Publishers are supposed to promote the book to help boost sales, but ask any author and you'll learn that simply doesn't happen anymore. Authors are expected to promote and sell their own books today. In fact, some publishers require a first-time author to guarantee a certain number of sales before even offering them a contract. If you have an audience big enough to sell the number of books required by a publisher, why do you need a publisher?

- **Editing and design:** This is where publishers normally excel, but there are so many freelance options available to self-publishers that it's relatively easy to create a beautiful book that looks as good as anything you can find in a bookstore.

- **Distribution:** This used to be a primary advantage of working with a publisher because it's difficult to get a self-published book on the shelves in a traditional bookstore on your own. But how many books are sold in a brick and mortar store anyway? Even if you earn placement in a store, chances are the book will only be available for a month or so. Self-published books can be sold through online channels, and that's sufficient. The historic distribution power of traditional publishers has been torpedoed by the popularity of online sales.

So why would anyone use a traditional publisher? Ego. To some people, it means something to have a literary agent and a book contract. But if you can put that aside, I'll contend that every significant reason to go through a traditional publisher has been neutralized today.

On the other hand, there are also some powerful advantages to self-publishing through a service like CreateSpace (which is owned by Amazon). Here are a few:

- **Revenue:** I make between 400 percent and 700 percent more per book when it's self-published (largely depending on the format: paper, electronic, or audio).

- **Flexibility:** You can revise your book and raise the price when you want to. I have more pricing power with Amazon than the mainstream publishers, who are limited by strict guidelines.

- **Ownership:** You retain all rights to your book instead of putting ownership in the hands of a company that might not exist in a few years.

- **Access:** Self-publishing is on-demand, meaning there are no inventory costs. I can order as many self-published books as I like for about $3.00 per copy. To buy a quantity of my books from a traditional publisher, I have to go through Amazon and pay the same price as you.

- **Speed:** If your book goes through a traditional publishing house, you can expect that it will be 9-18 months before it's printed. Through CreateSpace, I can turn in a manuscript and have a printed book in my hands, at my home, in about five days.

Also, consider that there are so many different formats for books today. Some authors are generating 10,000-word mini-books for $2.99. Some only go the electronic route or the audio route. The technology has opened up a lot of options.

Should you write a book? Only you can decide. I've given you an idea of the possibilities through this high-level view. There are extensive online resources to help you make an informed decision, and I hope you'll explore this more deeply.

Here's the beauty of our day: You no longer have to jump through hoops and pray that you'll be picked by a publisher. You can pick yourself ... and I hope you do.

Now let's turn to another opportunity to super-charge your presence: becoming a speaker.

Becoming a public speaker

I think you know how this section is going to start. What's the thing people fear more than death?

Public speaking!

In many ways, writing a book and becoming a speaker go hand in hand. It's difficult to become a professional paid speaker without a book. It's hard to promote a book without speaking about it.

Many people on the speaking circuit regard a book as their business card. A book is how people know you're qualified to speak to their group on your topic.

And with or without a book, becoming a speaker puts you on the fast track to becoming known.

Lee Odden, a founder of Minnesota-based marketing agency TopRank, started speaking for a very simple reason: He had to grow his business in a very competitive field.

"Eleven years ago, just the thought of public speaking terrified me," Lee said. "So why in the world did I say yes to a request to give a presentation about SEO and online PR to a group of 70 people at 7:30 in the morning at a library conference room? What could possibly compel me, a classic introvert, to stand up in front of a group of strangers and give a presentation? Simple. I had kids to feed.

"With a small business in need of customers and zero budget for marketing, I decided that if I could develop a personal brand and become known, I could attract buyers who were already interested in our services.

"I had tried everything else to build the business. Advertising. Cold calls. Dog and pony shows in front of distracted executives. I needed something else.

"I noticed other successful marketing consultants flush with work, giving presentations at events and attracting even more interested buyers. They also blogged and contributed articles to industry publications. They were recognized for their expertise and people trusted them. Those people referred these 'experts' to others in search of consulting. I saw that these individuals were successful because they were known. I knew I would have to face one of my worst fears and simply 'figure it out.'

"I'm still figuring it out, but the three things that have helped me become known in my field are blogging consistently, building an audience by generously helping others, and speaking. These three things worked together to help me land major brands as our clients."

If you want to develop a speaking career but you're paralyzed by fear, here's a link to a free test you can take to isolate the source of your fears and possibly resolve them: bit.ly/speakerfear.

The Top Five Reasons to Become a Public Speaker

1. It helps you connect to a real audience.

2. The act of creating a speech forces you to explain your points clearly.

3. Live speaking ignites awareness and networking.

4. It can become a direct income stream.

5. Speaking in front of an audience immediately imparts credibility and authority.

The Top Five Reasons NOT to Become a Public Speaker

1. It can be terrifying, at least in the beginning.

2. It might mean travel away from home, depending on your goals. (This can also be a positive if you like travel.)

3. If you're prone to illness, a speaking schedule is hard to reliably sustain.

4. Becoming an effective public speaker may require years of practice.

5. Putting together an effective and entertaining speech can be daunting.

I realize speaking isn't for everyone, but if you'd like to give it a try, you'll learn that few things in life beat the rewarding feeling of stepping off a stage to a hearty round of applause!

Creating your first speech

If you're like Lee Odden and find that pubic speaking is an essential part of becoming known, you'll need a few tips to get started. The first step is preparing your talk. Presentation strategist Tamsen Webster provides the following expert advice on how to craft your first speech:

1. Describe the situation for the talk.

- What's the event or situation for your talk? Thinking this through provides a context that makes it easier to be specific as you create your content.

- What length do you want the talk to be? What's the time slot you want or need to fill? This limitation establishes the amount of material you can cover. A rule of thumb: It takes 10 to 12 minutes to land a point effectively. An 18-minute TED-style talk typically provides one big idea, plus an opening and conclusion. The average 45-minute keynote lands three main points, with an opening and conclusion.

- Who's your *ideal* audience? What kind of people are they? What are their titles? What is their level of seniority? This thought exercise determines the audience's expertise, variety of opinions, and possibly, the level of formality the audience expects from you.

- What's the change you want to effect through your talk? What do you want them to think or do differently because of the talk? What is the goal?

2. Refine the core of the talk.

Think of your talk as a flow of five key concepts, which you'll present in order. If you can answer these questions in a complete sentence, you'll have the structure for your talk.

- What's the one thing the audience wants to achieve that your talk will ultimately address? By presenting that *goal,* you create desire, and desire precedes all change. The goal must be something the audience would readily agree they want, not something you have to convince them they want. This must be *their* goal, not the goal you desire for them.

- What's the underlying barrier to the audience's goal? This is the **problem** your talk will solve. It makes achieving the goal personally worth it ... and the pursuit of the goal a lot more interesting. The audience may or may not know they have this "real" problem, but it summarizes all the barriers they *do* see.

- What's the ONE thing your ideal audience member must understand to solve the problem? This is the *core idea.* The crucial concept unlocks why the problem exists and supports the change you want to propose.

- What's the single, high-level *change* the audience needs to solve the problem and achieve their goal? This is what all the actions boil down to.

- What *action,* or multiple actions, can the audience take to enact the change? If you have more than five, group them into a smaller number of categories.

3. Structure the talk by stringing those five sentences together.

Here's an example of a speech about customer communications. Let's put together the goal, problem, idea, change, and actions to structure a speech.

GOAL: "We all want to connect with the customers that matter most to us – and have the connection matter to them – but how can we achieve this when new tools and channels pop up all the time? How can we keep up with this rate of change?"

PROBLEM: "The real problem isn't the channels – it's what we're putting in them. We're not producing what people connect *with*."

IDEA: "You see, the 'new realities' of communication are really the *old* realities: the basics of why and how people decide to change."

CHANGE: "So what can we do? Because people connect to *meaning,* we need to design our communications around that – no matter the channel."

ACTION: "Creating meaning has three parts – substance, structure, and style – so let's talk about how we can design our communications using all three."

Conveniently, by stringing these core sentences together you've written a short description of your talk as well as a basic conclusion. Magic!

4. Fill in the details.

Now that you have an effective structure, let's connect those five ideas and smoothly move the audience from one section to the other through data, illustrations, and stories that support your points.

- Section 1: Establishing the goal and problem. If you've

done your homework, the audience agrees with the goal. Now fill them in on the data so they understand the problem.

- Section 2: Presenting the idea. You've brought them along to the point of understanding the problem. What stories and illustrations can you provide to support your idea and help them buy into it?

- Section 3: Laying out the action. What does the audience need to know to support the change and action required by your speech?

5. Add your personal style.

Go back and identify the examples, stories, data, and metaphors you'll use to support each of the main concepts in your presentation. Which of those might be a good way to open the talk? Look for something that frames the goal and/or problem.

While crafting your talk, it might help to write it out. Even if you never go back to the script, writing it out helps to (a) find the ideal language and (b) determine what doesn't fit, given the time you have to present. As a guide, there are about 135 to 150 words per minute. Your total word count will give you an idea of how close you are to your allotted time.

6. Punch it up.

Props, demonstrations, whiteboards/flip charts, and even sound bites can add interest and entertainment value to your talk. If you're using slides, share only one idea per slide (which means *no bullet points,* unless it's an agenda). Not every point you discuss needs a slide.

7. Rehearse ... and then rehearse some more.

It's impossible to over-rehearse. If you sound canned or

as if you've simply memorized your talk, you haven't re-hearsed enough. Rehearse until you know what you're saying so well that you're relaxed and in command.

How to start a speaking career

Now that you have a speech prepared and your confidence is building, let's take the show on the road. Here are some steps to build momentum as a professional speaker.

1. PREPARING A HOME BASE

If you don't already have a website to host your content, this would be a good time to create one. Unless you're a professional designer, don't make this a do-it-yourself project. If you want to establish yourself as an authoritative speaker, you need to look like an authoritative speaker. If you spend one dime on self-promotion, spend it on a great-looking website. It's your front door to the world.

At a minimum, your site should have an "About" page with your credentials, a speaking page with a description of your talk and ideal audience, and a contact page. This site can grow as your speaking career grows.

2. THINK LIKE AN ENTERTAINER

I once heard a podcast interview with a professional speaker that made a significant impact on my career. He said a great speech isn't a classroom lesson, it's a performance. Unfortunately, I can't remember his name, so I guess he didn't have *that* big of an impact on me, but I am forever indebted to his wisdom!

My unknown hero is exactly right. This new mindset permanently transformed my speaking approach from "teacher" to "entertainer."

Like a great performer, you need to rehearse. You need to know your lines and master your visual impact. You need to "block" your presence on the stage. You need to practice until you're sick of hearing yourself.

The goal of an entertainer is to be remembered, and that's your goal too if you want to be known. You probably won't be remembered for showing graphs and bullet points, but you might be remembered for a unique insight, a motivating story, and a lasting, emotional feeling of joy or inspiration.

After you construct your speech, scour it for any possible angle that can you can make more entertaining through a personal anecdote, a pause, an image, a sound, or a demonstration. Here are talks I remember:

- Brain researcher Jill Bolte Taylor brought a real human brain on the stage and held it in her hands during a TED talk.

- Business adviser Jay Baer spiced up a potentially boring talk on customer service by playing audio clips of actors reading real customer complaints and company responses.

- Entrepreneur Chris Brogan went to a thrift store and bought hundreds of superhero cards to pass out during his talk about finding your superpowers. I still have my card (Green Lantern!).

- Business leader Ann Handley brought a choir up on stage with her to sing about a key point.

- Activist and author Shereen El Feki compared an American Barbie doll and a Middle Eastern version to make a point about differing views of sexuality in the world.

- For one of my talks, I had a friend create a simple animated cartoon that I narrate from the stage. The audience always glows with smiling faces as they see my slides magically come to life and move about the screen.

You don't have to be this out-of-the-box to stand out, and you may not want to be if your speech demands gravitas. But in any speech you prepare, you should sweat over every word to deliver more than the audience expects.

3. START LOCAL

Look around your community for any group that requires speakers. A civic club. The chamber of commerce. A university classroom. Connect with any organization you can find and offer to speak for free.

Take every assignment you can get when you're starting out. Never say no. Repeat after me: The more you speak, the more you speak.

The speaking world is built on relationships. No matter how small an event, the person in charge of planning it wants to look good. And if they've heard from a trusted friend that you blew the audience away, the wheels of speaking momentum start to spin. The more you speak … the more you speak! At this point in your journey to be known, don't expect to be paid. Building awareness is your goal.

Every speech you make is an opportunity to learn something and refine your new craft. Maybe you'll be challenged to remain focused in a noisy room. Perhaps you'll learn to be flexible when your speaking time is unexpectedly cut in half (or doubled!). Maybe you'll stumble over a new way to use humor to connect to your audience.

Even after a decade as a speaker, I'm still learning every time out. At a major marketing event last year, the room's audio-visual system had a total collapse. I couldn't use any of my slides.

When it was time for the speech to start, I politely moved the panicked audio-visual people aside and told the room of 300 people they were about to experience "Mark Schaefer unplugged." It was quite a challenge to deliver a 45-minute speech without a safety net, but several people tweeted afterwards that it was the best speech at the event.

4. ESTABLISH SOCIAL PROOF

When we don't know the facts, we tend to look around our environment for clues that indicate truth. Consider this: At the scene of an accident, two people are shouting orders. One is dressed in a pizza delivery uniform and one is dressed in a lab coat like a doctor. Who do you listen to? The lab coat provides social proof of "authority." Maybe the lady in a lab coat is really a dentist and the guy in the pizza uniform is an off-duty emergency technician, but we often make decisions based on environmental clues.

This is an especially important concept in the online world because we're overwhelmed with so much information that we're hungry for clues to know who to trust.

Social proof can also establish your authority as a speaker. An important example of social proof would be testimonials from your talks posted on your website. Other forms of social proof would be a speaker's reel with highlights from your talks, a link to a video of a speech, and a list of where you've presented in the past.

5. BUILD MOMENTUM

A lot of new speakers seem obsessed with finding professional representation or working with a speaker's bureau. But until you can establish momentum by bringing in engagements on your own, they're probably not going to be interested in you.

What's the best way to get speaking engagements? To become known of course! See how this all works together? But it's true. Once you reach a certain threshold of visibility and popularity, you'll get more invitations and be able to raise your speaking fees, and only then might you get the attention of a professional bureau.

Actively marketing yourself as a speaker can diminish your perceived credibility. Part of the attraction of bringing in a noted speaker is that you're already established and known. I've learned through trial and error that selling yourself too hard may discount the value of what you do. The most effective strategy is to build momentum as I've outlined in this chapter:

1. Begin a journey to establish your brand and become known.

2. Say "yes" to every speaking opportunity that comes your way. That will lead to more invitations and referrals.

3. Ask people from events for testimonials to build your social proof.

4. Stay in touch with new contacts made at events and build them into your actionable audience.

If you're wildly successful and want to make speaking a major part of your career, you may eventually require an association with a bureau, but you can certainly build significant momentum on your own.

Writing a book and pursuing a speaking career are big steps, but I'd like you to consider these options, at least in year two or three of your journey to become known. Start looking for your own "big idea" – an idea that can become a pillar for a book, or a talk.

Congratulations! You've now completed the four steps in

the path to become known, and you've considered amplifying your efforts though a book or a speech.

Let's bring it all together now and meet a few inspiring people who have become known in their professional fields and are changing the world in some remarkable ways.

CHAPTER 9

Five Inspiring Stories of Known

"Opportunity is missed by most people because it is dressed in overalls and looks like work." – *Thomas Edison*

As we head into the last part of the book, I thought it would be helpful to tie things together and see how people have put the ideas of *KNOWN* into action. The fascinating stars of these stories overcame enormous obstacles to create a meaningful personal presence that helped them achieve their goals and even change the world.

You're going to have fun getting to know:

- Pete Matthew, an unconventional financial planner who got tired of making rich people richer

- Zander Zon, a musician who forged new territory in the competitive field of YouTube music videos with his craftsmanship and attention to detail

- Neale Godfrey, a gutsy banker who turned the publishing world on its head and became known for her ground-breaking children's books

- Felix Kjellberg, a college dropout who sold hot dogs on a street corner and became the first person to get 10 billion views on YouTube

- Jennifer James, a mom who's devoted to changing the world one blog post at a time

Shattering the mold in a regulated industry

I teach college courses at Rutgers University and typically have a few executives from industries like banking, pharmaceuticals, insurance, or wealth management in the room. Inevitably when the subject of building a personal brand comes up, somebody says, "But Mark you don't understand, I'm in a *regulated* industry!"

Without question, there are special considerations in industries with regulatory constraints. My first rule in life is, don't land in jail. By all means, listen to your lawyers. My second rule is, if regulations are keeping you from being competitive in your marketplace, figure it out ... like Pete Matthew did.

Pete is a financial planner in the quiet port village of Penzance in Cornwall, England. The economy of the ancient town has suffered over the years from the decline of its traditional industries of fishing, agriculture, and mining. It's slowly building new economic strengths in tourism and light industry, but through the transformation, Penzance has suffered from one of the highest unemployment rates in the country.

In other words, this is not a thriving environment for a personal financial planner. Pete was making a comfortable living, but becoming known outside of tiny Penzance seemed like a smart idea. And he had another reason for wanting to become known: He wanted to make a difference.

"I didn't want my legacy to be just helping rich people get richer," he said. "I wanted to make a dent in the universe. That sounds all very woo-woo and Zen when I think about it now, but when I had this realization, it was profound and I couldn't shake it from my mind. I wanted to find a way to accomplish something more.

"Throughout my career people had told me that I was good at explaining things, and that started to sink in. Financial planning is about helping clients visualize their long-term desires and then organizing their finances to meet those goals. I was beginning to see myself in the role of a teacher, and through the web I could reach more than one person at a time."

FINDING A SPACE

"I did some research and discovered a vacuum – there was nobody in the financial space creating any content like I had in mind, at least not in a consistent way," Pete said. "And so I began shooting videos, three per week, explaining how money works. It was an experiment, but I got better as time went on. I didn't get much of a reaction at first – it took 18 months for the first prospective client to approach me after watching my YouTube videos.

"The positive feedback I received encouraged me to keep going. I shot nearly 300 videos in two and a half years, and then after building an audience on YouTube, I created the Meaningful Money podcast in 2012. I messed around with that for a while, producing 12 episodes in six months, but nothing really happened until I became more consistent. When I published weekly, things started to take off.

"I think my 'place' is my ability to cut through jargon and technical speak and explain financial issues clearly and simply. In every single show, listeners have actionable takeaways.

"There's no doubt that being among the first in an unsaturated niche has helped me. And it's been fun. I'm comfortable with technology and enjoyed learning to do the recording, editing, and everything to produce my shows."

Pete's show has become a global sensation, averaging 1,000 downloads a day, a significant number for a podcast of any kind. He attributes his success to the helpful, original content and the endurance to keep at it.

"The consistency of your content is the key to building an audience, especially early on in the process," he said. "I tell anyone thinking about starting a blog, podcast, or video that if they can't think of at least 50 subject lines or topics, they probably shouldn't start, or they should switch to a different field. People ask me all the time if I'll ever run out of things to say, and I laugh! I get asked questions by my audience all the time, so there's a limitless supply of material."

STAYING OUT OF JAIL

"I never had any reservations about the view of the legal regulators," Pete said. "The rules around what you can and can't say are easily interpreted in my view. It's a very different thing to say, 'saving for retirement is a good idea' rather than 'here's a great new product by Fidelity.' Advisers ask me all the time about compliance, but in my view you'd have to be an idiot to fall foul of the rules!

"Taking a practical approach in a regulated industry has helped me get ahead and stay ahead of competitors. Sure, there are other people attempting to produce content in the financial space now, but it's reworked to death by compliance departments and becomes so homogenized and boring that it is of zero value.

"In the last two or three years my content has become a major source of new client inquiries for me. But by far the biggest benefit is the feedback I receive. My listeners tell me they've taken action as a result of my content. They've risen out of debt and turned their financial lives around. I love that. THIS is my purpose, and this is why I continue to pour my soul into the podcast."

A Bass of a Different Color

Every minute of every day, a staggering 300 hours of video are uploaded to YouTube. The channel is immensely popular – and saturated with artists trying to become the next Rhianna or Justin Bieber. The idea of a young man making his living by recording videos of himself playing a bass guitar alone in a room seems impossible. But that's exactly what London-based Zander Zon has achieved.

Zander uses the high register of his bass to create original melodies and unexpected soundscapes that bring out the clear, bell-like tones of his instrument. He's become known for his ambitious covers of famous songs and artists. Zander's music has an aching beauty, whether it's a pop cover from Adele or a traditional piece like "Scarborough Fair." His preparation and attention to every note and tone is remarkable. Look up his cover of the theme from "Star Wars" on YouTube. It's hard to believe all that sound is coming from one bass!

But even the greatest bass players on the planet haven't had the millions of views Zander has received. To be known and respected so widely for videos of one man playing one instrument is remarkable.

As a boy, Zander was a cello player, but when his friends needed a bass player for their new rock band, he picked up the instrument and never put it down.

"There was a massive amount of practice and hard work," he told me. "I sometimes would play bass for 12 hours a day. By the time I released my first video on YouTube in 2008, I had been playing music for almost 20 years. I'd put in at least 10,000 hours of practice by that point.

Zander certainly knew both his gift and his passion. But was it sustainable? How could he build fans for an instrument generally regarded as part of the rhythm section, the anonymous background of the band? The key to his success was taking a significant personal risk and jumping into a new space – the emerging world of personal music videos.

TAKING THE RISK

"Despite feeling fairly confident with my craft and having lots of encouragement from friends and family, I had a deep fear of uploading my music to the internet. These days it's commonplace for artists to upload to YouTube, but back then very few musicians were doing it. I was apprehensive about putting myself out there, and I was fearful of any negative feedback I might receive.

"When I was 24, my father was diagnosed with cancer. This was such a shock to me, and it changed the way I thought about my life. I began to understand that my life was short. I needed to live more boldly, without regret, and I became more willing to seize the moment. Uploading a video to YouTube seemed easy compared to what my father was going through. So I did it."

The pain and emotion of Zander's family tragedy came through in his music, and he learned to add his personality to his music. "I want to create content that forms an emotional connection," he said. "When I experience art that really moves me, it's a very special experience. So anytime I'm writing or arranging music, my purpose is to create something that gives people a similar experience. The emotions vary – from joy and happiness to melancholy and even awe. I think translating this emotion to music is what makes me stand out."

SUCCESS IN THE DETAILS

"I'm a perfectionist," Zander said. "I'm driven to constantly improve each song. I spend hours evaluating my arrangements, the tone of my instrument, and the quality of the video. A few years ago I invested in an HD camera, and that's become the norm on YouTube. I've also learned how to create videos with multiple camera angles and bought some new instruments. All this attention to detail actually increases the degree of creative freedom I have, which makes what I'm doing more fun and adds value and diversity to my videos."

From the beginning, Zander had a positive reception from the YouTube community and his audience grew quickly. The challenge is earning that audience over and over again with every video.

"There are many people creating content who have one hit or one big idea," he said. "The goal then has to be sustainability. Sustaining excellence is the key to success. I don't know if you're ever truly 'there' on YouTube. Even premium YouTubers are still trying to think of ways to stay relevant so they can continue what they're doing. There are hundreds of hours of video uploaded to YouTube every minute. That's the new competition. You can never stay still, it's always on to the next thing.

"And of course there are lots of forms of success. I'm not on YouTube to make a lot of money. I'm in it because of the feeling I get from self-expression and connecting with people. Making music makes me feel alive and gives me great joy. I want my music to make other people feel the same way. The greatest gift is having an audience willing to give their time to experience my art. I feel so grateful for that."

Getting to know Zander through his videos has inspired me. Of course his music is utterly amazing, but what I respect about him most is the effort he devotes to staying relevant, securing his place in the hearts of his fans, and remaining known.

"The main reason I am known – and this holds true for

other stars on YouTube as well – is I am willing to put in an insane amount of work."

Knocking down a lifetime of barriers

Neale Godfrey is a woman who has knocked down barriers throughout her life. And to become known as a children's book author, well, she literally had to use brute force.

As one of the first female executives at The Chase Manhattan Bank in the 1980s, Neale was a business pioneer. She is a teacher, a philanthropist, and a single mother. But what she's known for is teaching children and families about money. How she became known in that niche is a fascinating example of combining an interest in money and banking with her values – empowering disadvantaged people to take control of their financial lives.

Neale Godfrey's "Only I ..." is to "serve as the financial voice for Baby Boomers, millennials, and their offspring." In fact, Neale created an entire category of literature based on this niche.

"I wanted to be a bank president one day," Neale said, "but felt I hit the glass ceiling in those days at Chase. So I was given an opportunity to become president of the First Women's Bank. I know it's hard to believe now, but before the Fair Credit Act was passed, it was difficult for a woman to get credit in her own name.

"What I realized is that many women had not been taught how to manage money when they were young. So I wanted to break this cycle. I wanted my own children to learn how to handle money. We traipsed around every bookstore in New York City and couldn't find one book that taught children about money!

"At this point, my daughter said, 'Well, Mommy, why don't

you write the book?' I guess I looked a little dumbfounded and astounded by the idea, and she said, 'What's the matter, are you scared?'

"And I said I wasn't ... but of course I was. I started thinking about this idea and it really did align with my core values. This book was so needed. Somebody had to write this book. Why not me?"

Neale researched the topic and found that people could be logically grouped by how they handled money. So she created a fanciful cartoon world where characters in her book demonstrated both the good and bad money habits children can observe in real life. After months of work, her book was completed. Now, what to do with it?

BECOMING KNOWN IN A NEW FIELD

Although she had a successful business career and was well-respected in the banking industry, in the book world Neale Godfrey was a nobody. She lacked the star power usually required to land a book deal.

"This was long before the days of social media and self-publishing," she said. "So for me to become known, I had no choice but to get the attention of a traditional New York book publisher. I was confident and excited about the idea. This was the first book of its kind. We could own the whole category! But the book publisher couldn't see it that way. They said, there are no books in the category, so there must be no interest in it! I felt like I was shut down before I even started.

"I worked for about a year to demonstrate the need for the book but still, they wouldn't accept the idea. Nothing I said would get through to them because they were so risk-averse. At this same time, I had been working with at-risk kids – through the Institute for Youth Entrepreneurship in Harlem – and I was so moved and motivated to teach these kids that they could have control of their financial future. But nobody would publish that book. I had to do something quite dramatic and forceful or I would never see this vision through. So I bought a small publishing house. And I said, 'We're going to publish this book.' And they said, 'We're not sure about this idea.' And I said, 'Yes you are because I can fire you!' So, we published the book!"

THE BRAND IGNITES

"The book sold 50,000 copies, which is a lot for a children's book. So I went back to the big publishing house. Now they could finally see there was a need for this kind of content! They agreed to publish a new book, *Money Doesn't Grow on Trees,* and it became a huge best-seller.

"After the book came out, my daughter answered the phone, turned to me, and said it was Oprah. Of course I thought it was my friend pretending to be Oprah, but in fact it was Oprah! I ended up appearing on her show, and I sold a million books. I continued to appear on her show for four and a half years."

Since then, Neale has published nearly 30 books and has expanded her content reach to workshops, speeches, online tutorials, and even video games that teach kids money skills. She has appeared on CNN, *Good Morning America,* and *The Today Show.*

While Neale's story is a great example of finding a sustainable interest based on a passion mashed up with a core value, there are other lessons from Neale that are common to many of the success stories in this book:

- She found her place, an uncontested topical niche teaching kids and families about managing their money.

- She worked extremely hard to get attention for her project and to prove the worth of her idea. She wasn't an overnight success.

- She became known through her unique, high-quality, helpful content.

- She demonstrated real grit by finding a way to publish her book when she was rejected by the industry gatekeepers.

Finally, there was something beyond mere money that drove Neale to succeed and be known. "I once gave a speech at a large corporation," she said. "And a woman came up to me after my talk. She said 'You don't remember me, but I was one of the women you helped get off welfare and get through high school.' Well, not only did she make it through high school, she had graduated from college and was now a senior vice president at this company.

"When you have a moment like that, you know you're doing the right work in your life."

From hot dog vendor to YouTube's hottest star

Unless you're really into gaming, you probably don't recognize the name Felix Kjellberg. In 2010, Felix started a YouTube channel featuring his own funny commentary while he played video games. In fact, making these silly videos became his obsession. He dropped out of college to do it full-time with no idea of how he would actually make a living. His parents became so infuriated that they withdrew their financial support until he got a job or went back to school.

Undeterred, Felix sold hotdogs from a street corner to scrape by and maintain his gaming lifestyle. Just when it seemed like it couldn't get any worse, he was locked out of his YouTube account and had to start over, this time with a new name: PewDiePie (he explained that "pew" represents the sound of lasers and "die" means death.)

Although this was the era when many YouTube stars were getting their start, there weren't many who loved gaming as much as Felix. Within a year, his channel had 60,000 subscribers, and in just 12 months, that audience had exploded to 700,000 fans. Within 24 months of opening his new account, Felix had a worldwide community of more than 2 million subscribers and was the first person on YouTube to eclipse 10 billion views.

The first time I saw a PewDiePie video I was mystified. Most of the screen was a video game except for a small box in the corner, which showed Felix playing. Every few seconds, he'd make a joke, screech, unleash a string of expletives, or react to events with an exaggerated facial expression. I remember thinking, what the heck is this?

But the more I viewed his channel, the more I understood why "Pewds," who now has nearly 50 million subscribers, is the most-watched person in YouTube history. He's charming, raw, and funny, and he knows how to entertain. He essentially pioneered a new content form – commentary entertainment. It's so personal and human that it's almost like being on a Skype call with the guy.

In addition to creating game-based videos, PewDiePie became legendary by maintaining a tireless connection to his fans through public appearances. He built a multimedia company around his videos, and his eight-figure salary exceeds the income of many mainstream movie stars.

Felix is a bit of an outlier in this book because he is by far the most famous person in these pages. PewDiePie has been included on *Time* magazine's list of the 30 most influential people on the internet. But I wanted to include him because even somebody with that kind of fame followed the same four steps that I outline in this book, although he might not have realized it at the time!

His place was irreverent, game-based videos. His space was

"commentary entertainment," which was new at the time he began. He published his content consistently every day for years and tirelessly connected with his fans as equals.

On the surface, it might be difficult to discern whether Felix has a "purpose" beyond being a goofball. But his extreme internet influence has provided a powerful forum for him to bring attention to exploitive practices by YouTube. He's become an authoritative voice of reform on the social channel and paved the way for fairer monetization for other YouTube stars.

As you've seen, nearly every person in this book has a purpose beyond selling stuff. But there's one woman who has taken it to an even higher level ...

The world-changer

Jennifer James has become known ... very well known. She's been featured in national magazines and television shows and routinely pops up on lists of the most influential women in America. But her goal isn't to leverage her influence to start a speaking career, make a million dollars, or even have a viral video. Jennifer is obsessed with one idea: Change the world, one blog post at a time.

Jennifer was already successful as the founder of the world's largest community for moms who blog when one trip to Africa spun her life in an entirely new direction.

"The catalyst for my work started with a trip to Kenya in 2012," she said. "It was my first trip to Africa to observe the work being done by USAID, the Center for Disease Control, and many brave individuals who work at hospitals and clinics. That trip changed my life! I had never seen that level of abject poverty and the lack of basic healthcare that is ubiquitous in developing countries.

"I felt a bit overwhelmed by it all, but then I had an epiphany. Global issues about poverty and education, world hunger, and sex trafficking don't need to be solved by me. They can be solved when intelligent people bring solutions to the table and then bloggers like me and my friends move those ideas through the internet. Spreading ideas – that's where the power of change happens.

"Through my blog, I had already created a community of 18,000 moms. For years, mom bloggers have worked well with consumer brands, and I had a gut feeling that mom bloggers were also ready to connect for social good. Could I bring them together around these social causes? I went to the bloggers from my blog community and asked them if they wanted to be founding members of Social Good Moms. 400 women signed up in one day. Now, there are over 3,000.

"Since we began, our impact has been felt around the world. Every day, ordinary people are learning about global health and international development because our members spread the word about big issues like maternal and child health, global malnutrition, and pressing issues concerning women and girls.

"Many people believe that digital actions for social causes aren't as effective as other philanthropic actions like writing checks or serving the homeless at a local soup kitchen. Clicks and shares for charity have been painted in a bad light, and it's assumed that they aren't really effective. But I've maintained that social actions are not mindless ones. Even though social actions are scanned by people and acted upon quickly, it doesn't mean that they're done without thought. Social actions on the web are just one piece of a complicated puzzle that builds toward action. Action begins with awareness and education about big issues people would otherwise ignore.

"Busy moms don't normally have time to work at a charity event. They may be on a budget and struggle to feed their own families, let alone others. I simply saw a problem and solved it for busy moms who want to do more. I've given them an opportunity to help make a sizable impact.

"My goal when I started this community was modest. Even I've been surprised by the sheer number of collective actions we've taken and the amount of awareness we bring to issues that matter the most in our lifetime."

The idea of bringing people together for social good isn't a new concept. But Jennifer is unique because she has sustained and grown an effort over many years. By fostering a community through content and sustaining it through consistent connection, she's built momentum for her ideas where many others have failed.

"The internet is extremely noisy!" she said. "I knew when I started Social Good Moms that to make this work, I had to be heard in a unique way. I had to have a clear online voice, and I had to present it in an innovative way. I had to be authentic and practice what I preached for other moms to follow my example and use social media for good.

"I learned over the years that if you don't have consistency you really can't build a community. People need to know you're reliable so they feel good about being part of a winning team. Thousands of Social Good Moms around the world work together for collective actions because they trust the source: the bloggers that they routinely read or follow on social media.

"Consistency can be a burden or it can be really fun and productive. For me, it's the latter, because consistency means bettering the world and helping those in need. No one can make positive change in a vacuum and no one can create change without consistency.

"One thing I noticed was that many nonprofits and NGOs had difficulty speaking online to ordinary people who rarely stop to think about pressing global issues. The value I provide is bridging that gap with a community of moms, the audience

I know the best. I'm not sure if I can say that 'only I' could create a vibrant online community of Social Good Moms, but I do believe I've done it in a way the world had not seen before."

Interviewing nearly 100 people for this book has been a source of great inspiration for me, and I hope these people have had a positive impact on you, too. We have some more remarkable people to meet in the pages ahead, but first let's take a hard look at some practical realities. What if you desperately want to be known, but nothing seems to be working out? What are your options? How do you know if it's time to adjust, pivot ... or quit?

CHAPTER 10

Pivots and Grit

"Fall seven times and stand up eight." – Japanese proverb

As you've learned by now, this isn't a book filled with unicorns and rainbows. It's a practical book with grounded advice from real people who have struggled and won, fallen and persisted. If you've worked for a while on the path to become known and still have some doubts, I'm offering this chapter to you as a ... repair manual of sorts.

What if you're working your tail off and can't seem to make things happen? In this chapter, I'll help you answer these questions:

- Is this the right time for you to become known?

- How do you overcome the fear of starting?

- How do you measure progress to know whether your effort is working?

- When should you be patient, and when do you know it's time to quit?

- How can you pivot and make adjustments that might turn things around?

This is a chapter of straight talk and support based on the realities of this world. Let's start by looking at the great non-negotiable resource: time.

Chronos and *Kairos*

The ancient Greeks had two words for time: *chronos,* the tick-tock chronological time we're familiar with, and *kairos,* which means "the right time."

Time is your biggest enemy in the effort to become known. Not just the *chronos,* how much time you're putting into it, but the *kairos* ... is this the right time to do it? Let's look at both aspects of success.

There's a lot of hype on the web today devoted to the concept of hustle, which is another way of saying you're using your time obsessively in pursuit of a single goal. In fact, one guru suggests that you "suffocate all else in your life" in pursuit of the hustle, implying that your friends, family, and hobbies have to take a back seat for you to be truly successful. How many people can live like that?

At the risk of sounding grounded, I don't think that sort of obsession is healthy or sustainable. Perhaps that degree of single-mindedness is an attempt to fill a boundless need for validation that no amount of hustle will satisfy.

Becoming known requires consistent hard work, but you don't have to suffocate the rest of your life to do it. The successful people in this book have families, hobbies, and charitable activities they support outside the hustle. If you sacrifice family, and even your health, to rise to the top of your industry, I might question if the goal is truly worth achieving.

Nobody in this book was an overnight success. Their course was slow and steady, in every case. So instead of hustle, let's focus on what's truly paramount: commitment and endurance.

How much time do you need to devote to this activity? Unfortunately, there's no uniform answer that applies to every person and every situation. The time needed to achieve a breakthrough depends on

- **Your current status** – For example, if you're already respected in your niche, you have a shorter climb ahead of you.

- **Your content form** – The amount of time it takes for Isadora Becker to prepare one of her film-themed YouTube cooking videos is far more than what it takes construction worker Shawn Van Dyke to prepare an inspirational quote for Instagram. Long-form blogger Avinash Kaushik of Google may work for weeks on one of his epic blog posts, while Tom Fishburne creates a funny business cartoon in just an hour or two.

- **Your competition** – Most of the time your strategy is dictated by the competition. The rules of engagement are determined by the requirements of the battle.

So, there is no standard answer. But if you've determined your *place* and *space,* and you're seeking some guidelines to get started, consider this:

- Spend at least three hours per week creating your preferred type of content.

- Devote about an hour per week to igniting your content through promotion and distribution.

- Use at least one hour each week to engage with your audience and influencers.

Five hours a week ... at least. That's a lot of time. Success may require that degree of devotion, applied consistently for years. Let's review some of the case studies we've already covered, from the perspective of the *chronos* sort of time:

- Antonio Centeno created short fashion videos every day for 200 days to learn how to do it well. And then he started a new challenge: 1,000 videos in 1,000 days.

- Lorraine Loots has created a piece of miniature art every day of her life since 2013.

- Rand Fishkin of Moz produced his "whiteboard videos" for two years before they gained traction, and three years before the audience equaled his blog content success.

Are you at a point in your life where you can put in that much work? To answer that, let's turn to the concept of *kairos*.
Is this the right time for you to become known?

Kairos

One of the exasperating things about our culture today is the prevailing attitude that if you're not remarkable, you're a failure. Perhaps you're expecting me to say ...
You can do it!
All you need is hustle!
You were made to be remarkable, so stop making excuses!
Here's the wrong reason to want to become known: because you've been suckered in by the endless "manifestos" about

dreaming your way to success and adventure. Over and over we're pounded with these self-help rainbow bombs until we begin to believe that if we're not dreaming our way to a better life, there must be something wrong with us. The guilt trip might start with a Facebook meme like this:

"Life is either a daring adventure or nothing at all."

After puffy mantras like this, people may chime in with comments like, "Amen!" "YESSSSS!" and "This is so true! This is what I needed to hear!"

It's easy to see why people begin to feel inadequate when everybody they know seems to be in the process of becoming remarkable.

You can be a great and worthy person without writing your manifesto, living out of your box, or daring to be a failure. Sometimes life gets in the way and the best you can do is deal with it in an unremarkable, yet heroic, manner. For example:

- My college friend has had a long career in the military. His job does not require him to develop a personal brand or a blog. He doesn't dwell on what he needs to do to become remarkable. His job is to keep his country safe, and that is admirable.

- My friend Jayme Soulati had a dream to become known as a thought leader in the field of public relations, write a book, and join the speaking circuit. She started down that path, but as the single mom of an active 10-year-old, Jayme had to dramatically reduce her focus on personal branding in order to simply take care of life. "I'm the breadwinner for my family," she said. "My time is no longer entirely mine … but my time will come."

- One of my business colleagues put his career on hold to raise two kids with special needs. He and his wife are exhausted and stressed every day. They have no time to create, innovate, or promote their lives on Snapchat. At the end of the day they simply collapse in exhaustion. It's not his *kairos,* his time to be known.

Centering your life on a "Living Your Dream" manifesto can be a shallow, elitist, and self-absorbed way to go through life. And yet, that message is pervasive in our culture.

Success is personal

I've long admired Paul Roetzer, the founder and leader of the PR20/20 digital agency. Paul is superstar material – brilliant, charismatic, visionary, and hard-working. But he's made a decision to NOT become known ... and that makes me admire him even more. Here's Paul's view:

> I started thinking about becoming known in my industry – what does it take to build a personal brand? To do that, you have to constantly innovate, you have to come up with the next idea, travel to see your audience, blog almost every day ... and for me it became this interesting challenge. Once you get big, how do you handle it? If you have 100,000 people following you, everybody wants a piece of you and you need to engage with your audience, but at some point, you lose that ability to engage. It's a scale issue for me.

> It's almost like being a musician. They put out a record (their content) and then you go see them in concert. But then if they don't put out another record, the audience goes away. In our industry, it seems like you should create something every single day. It's a constant battle to stay on top.

There are some people who have done it very, very well. Can you sustain a career with that? At the point I was looking at this, I was 34. I was young. I had to make a decision. Am I willing to constantly travel, speak, and aggressively build an audience? For me, the decision was "no" because I had my first child on the way. I wasn't going to miss my kids growing up in pursuit of money and fame.

To make a decision to be known, it really ties to purpose. Why do we do what we do? I gave up working nights and weekends the day my daughter was born, and I've never looked back with one moment of regret.

Success is personal. The value of finding your purpose and staying true to it is universal and profound.

I'm not saying you shouldn't follow your dreams. I'm not saying you shouldn't be remarkable or fight every day to realize your promise and potential. You should. But I'm letting you off the hook for one moment to let you know that if this isn't the right time for you to devote a significant amount of your time to becoming known, well, that's OK.

If this isn't your *kairos,* you are still worthy. Your time to become known will come. It is honorable to live a life that transcends self-interest.

Is the *kairos* right for you?

Overcoming fear and imposter syndrome

If this is your time to become known, then normally the next challenge you face is the fear of starting.

I once read that we are all living in a "primordial soup of dreams." I like that characterization. Like a new being rising from the ooze, we all have the chance to recreate ourselves into something bold and new. But you do have to take the first step out of the soup.

Nobody is born a thought leader. It's something you need to earn in the mind of your audience, slowly over time. You should approach the process of becoming known with humility and respect to those who came before you.

One of my heroes since I was a boy has been the American patriot, scientist, philosopher, and diplomat Benjamin Franklin. He once wrote that in order to succeed as a leader we need to cultivate humility and imitate individuals like Jesus and Socrates. Franklin understood that to be great at something, you need to be humble and imitate the successful qualities of other great leaders. It was his genteel way of saying "fake it until you make it."

Don't worry about having all the answers. Imitate what you want to be until you actually become it.

By now, you've spent time identifying a strategy to move forward. Perhaps you have a grainy idea of what your future could look like. Now walk toward that future step by step.

When I started blogging nearly a decade ago, I had a rough idea of where I was going, but I was no expert in digital marketing, social media, or blogging. Since then, I've written entire books on those subjects and I'm invited to do consulting and training all over the world. I've earned it. But I started at zero, with complete humility, and became successful by reading, researching, and studying the success of others.

I found the pioneering bloggers and digital leaders of my day and patiently uncovered what made them great. I realized I was doing almost everything wrong, but I was willing to look at my mistakes as lessons on the journey. Progress was painfully slow, but I now attract the same number of readers to my site in a month as I did in my first two years of blogging combined! Becoming known is a process that involves perseverance and self-driven growth.

I love this quote from one of my favorite radio personalities, Ira Glass, host of the radio show "This American Life."[1] "Even the stuff you're really good at, you're not necessarily really good at right away."

Ira's program, syndicated to more than 500 radio stations and with millions of listeners online, ushered in a new wave of journalistic storytelling. But was he always that good? No. "The key thing, I think, is to just force yourself through the work, to put yourself in a position where you have to turn out product," he said. "That forces the skills to come."

The delicate dance between skills and progress is the hardest part of this process. You need to create content that adds value while you're still in the process of learning. Your confidence will be shaken, you'll fail, and you'll question your abilities. Even the best in the business have their confidence upset at times.

The beauty of faking it

Author and business leader Ann Handley has written about this idea of *impostor syndrome* a number of times. "Impostor syndrome is a feeling that despite getting accolades, professional recognition, and maybe tons of money, glory, and success, you nonetheless feel like you're tricking everyone and you're actually not very good at anything," she said.

"I saw a chart on Buzzfeed[2] that made me laugh," she said. "On one side it said 'What you think you are: A hot crazy fire mess of a person who disappoints important people.' On the other side, it said 'Who others think you are: Cool and fine.'

"When I posted this chart on Facebook, a barrage of friends chimed in, many agreeing how they feel strangely out of their depth – whether real or imagined – as a true life struggle.

"And many of those people are incredibly talented, driven, accomplished, and successful. So why do accomplished people sometimes feel like impostors? Probably because at some point ... they were.

"Early in my career, I worked as a news reporter in a busy business newsroom; literally though, I was just pretending to be a news reporter because I had no idea what I was doing.

"Age, time, successes, and failures have greatly diminished my sense of impostor syndrome. But, every once in a while, the familiar doubt still rises within me. But I've come to embrace it as less of a handicap and more of a good thing, for three reasons:

1. Impostor syndrome is evidence that you're still growing as a professional and as a person.

2. Impostor syndrome is evidence that you're not an arrogant jerk.

3. Impostor syndrome can be a useful divining rod or guide telling you that the new path you're taking (in life or career) just might be the wrong one.

"So, impostor syndrome is useful. It's an asset – a tiny critic that prods me to produce my best work and that keeps me from being an arrogant, insufferable know-it-all."

It's easy to assume that industry leaders like Ann had some sort of genius master plan, a straight and secure path that rocketed them to the top. In a haze of fear about our own choices, we assume successful people didn't face those same insecurities or ever take a step that led them astray. But they did – often.

If you start creating content, you'll be better at it six months from now. It will come more easily, you'll be more comfortable, and your skills will improve. But here's a guarantee: You'll never experience that euphoric feeling of progress and growing confidence if you never start.

When is it time to pivot?

Becoming known is not a linear process. You'll stumble along the way. Repeatedly.

In fact, the only way you're going to make it is to fail. So don't be afraid of it. Adopt a mindset that accepts missteps as part of the path to success.

Embracing this attitude is easier said than done, however.

Seth Godin, one of the most well-known and accomplished marketing experts on the planet, once explained that he removed comments from his blog because he became obsessed with every negative remark. Business advisor Gary Vaynerchuk said that no matter how much success he's had, the negative comments still hurt.

Being known doesn't mean you're not human.

Similarly, most of us are built to avoid a venture that might fail because that would hurt. I've acknowledged in this chapter that sometimes life gets in the way of your goals. But I also want to challenge you to be sure you're not using "life" as an excuse when the real obstacle is fear of failure. Failure is never the end of the story. Mistakes and even epic blunders are part of your life university. As John C. Maxwell put it, sometimes you win, sometimes you learn.

My graduate school professor and mentor Peter Drucker once told me that every entrepreneur fails – and in fact, must fail. "But no entrepreneur aims to fail, and takes every effort to buffer themselves from failure. It's OK to fall down. Just don't fall down a hole so deep you can't get out of it!"

How do you know whether a failure along the way is a lesson to learn from or a sign from the universe that you're heading in the wrong direction entirely?

Success rarely comes in a blinding rush. It comes gradually, like the changing of the seasons. You can't stand in front of a maple tree and observe how its leaves change to their brilliant autumn colors. But week by week, the change does occur and the momentum builds. One way to determine if it's time to pivot or quit is to actually measure that momentum.

When it comes to quantifying a soft concept like "thought leadership," or personal branding momentum, there are four measures that can help you determine whether you're trending up or down.

1. The first is a measure of **awareness.** Awareness can be quantified through easy measurements like social media mentions, "likes," site traffic, and the number of times your content is being shared. Are people more aware of you this month compared to last month? This year compared to last year? A growth in awareness is a leading indicator of positive personal results over time.

2. The second measure is **inquiries.** If your reputation as a thought leader is being established, you would expect to see this show up as signs of interest in your professional work. Record inquiries of any kind – organizations who want you to speak, contribute content, provide advice, answer a question, offer a recommendation – all signs that your reputation is improving. Tallying these inquiries month by month provides an effective indicator of momentum.

3. **Money** is an excellent sign of the mounting value of your skill. People will only give you money if they're receiving value, so even if revenue isn't your end goal, money is a great source of honest feedback that your skills are appreciated.

4. The fourth measure should be connected to **your per-**

sonal goals. Why do you want to become known? Is it to achieve recognition? Share your ideas more broadly? Reach some professional milestone? Establish more flexibility in your worklife? Only you can determine if you're reaching these intrinsic goals and if your work is providing personal reward.

The simplest way to think about measurement is, are you seeing indicators of continuous progress? As long as you're moving forward and enjoying the work, keep on going because it may take years for your brand to finally tip. I wish there was a way to shorten this process or provide some sort of guarantee, but this path is rarely quick or assured.

Is it time to quit? As long you're still seeing measurable signs of progress, NO! Here's a case study to show how you can apply these measures in the real world.

Case study: Measuring progress

"I'm loving your *Tao of Twitter* book," John Espirian wrote to me in an email. "I'm learning a lot!" For an author like myself, there are no sweeter words! And so, John immediately had my attention.

John is an experienced technical writer based in Wales, and through our social media connections, I learned that he was re-evaluating his career path. He had dreams of being recognized as an authority in his industry, he wanted to write a book, and he hoped to be invited to speak at conferences one day.

In other words, John needed to become known.

While he had received many professional awards throughout his distinguished career, John was ready to break out and take his life and business to a new level. He believed that building a profound presence on the web would create a network that could help him realize his goals and lead to new business opportunities.

John already had some legitimate strengths going for him:

- He had a wealth of experience as a technical writer.

- He had started to create relevant, business-related content in the form of blog posts and instructional videos.

- He understood the power and potential of social media.

- He knew it would take a long time to build an effective digital presence and was willing to be patient, even if it took years to achieve his goals.

This was a great starting point, but some key elements were missing.

First, John lacked a distinctive *place* and *space*. He identified his sustainable interest as "I help ideas grow." The problem with this statement (as you know by now) is that it's far too generic. That statement could be the tagline of a management consultant, a fertilizer company, or a banker. John was frustrated that people struggled to understand what he did ... and one of the reasons for this is that he had not specifically defined his place in an accurate, unique, and memorable way.

In a phone conversation, John came alive when he started describing his passion for helping people understand how communications was changing. He had experimented a lot with video and was convinced that this was the future of technical writing. Now, that's an interesting idea, isn't it? "The future of words" seemed to hold a lot more potential than "helping ideas grow." I wondered aloud ... Who owns the space for the future of writing? Clearly, this could be a sustainable interest for John, but how big is the niche? Does he have enough room to maneuver? Is there a large and actionable audience?

As a first assignment, I recommended a few of the exercises in this book to help further define John's sustainable interest and his space. We thought we were on to something with this "future of writing" angle, and the potential space – all content creators on earth – was huge.

Once John zeroed in on this more defined "voice," he had to revisit the type of content he'd produce to support his effort to become known.

To identify a possible space to occupy, we Googled some of the keywords on his topic. One thing was clear: The web was overrun with "hygiene" how-to content. But with John's extensive experience, he might be able to stand out through longer, more in-depth thought leadership "hub" pieces.

My second challenge for John was to define his personal view of success. He wanted to be known as a thought leader in his field but didn't know how to measure something as soft as "authority." We decided that progress needed to be measured through indicators of awareness, opportunity, and ultimately, financial benefits.

John was smart enough to recognize it might take several years of brand-building before those benefits began to be accrue, and he committed to begin.

Applying the measures of momentum

Realigning his direction and creating a focused effort on becoming known had an immediate impact on John's life and business. He had been slogging through his career but was energized now that he had a plan instead of just an idea. He worked quickly on all elements of his strategy to become known and overhauled his content plan by creating a new subscription newsletter called "Espresso" that featured in-depth hub content.

Within three months, his awareness measures had increased by 500 percent. There were bright indicators of momentum:

- He was featured in a video interview.

- He became involved in a UK professional organization.

- He was interviewed on an industry podcast.

- He received an invitation to appear on a second podcast.

- He was invited to create a training course with a trusted colleague.

- He started working with many new influencers who were helping him build his audience.

- He was featured in a blog post about Twitter success strategies.

- He was offered seven new freelance job opportunities.

- He received a request to create guest posts at a prestigious industry site.

- He got his first invitation to speak on a conference panel.

By employing some of the audience-building techniques from Chapter 7, John's Twitter following increased by 300 relevant individuals, a ten-fold acquisition rate compared to where he was when he began. The subscriptions to his new newsletter stood at 85, an impressive start for a beginning blogger in a crowded niche.

These are all powerful indicators that John is heading in the right direction. He's becoming known! By recording these types of accomplishments month by month, he recognizes progress, which is encouragement to keep going.

Not all these accomplishments are quantitative (something you can count, like money, a sales lead, or a new contract), but that's OK. You also need to embrace qualitative measures such as awareness and new connections as legitimate indicators of progress.

And as long as you have momentum, you must persevere.

Will John reach his goals? It may take years to know for sure because ultimately success requires vicious consistency, patience, and grit.

Case study: Grit

The *Oxford Dictionary* defines grit as "Courage and resolve; strength of character."

Grit in its many forms has been a hot topic in recent years, fueled by best-selling books like Malcolm Gladwell's *Outliers: The Story of Success* (which propelled the "10,000 hours of work" idea into the language of popular culture) and Charles Duhigg's *The Power of Habit: Why We Do What We Do in Life and Business,* about changing behavioral patterns through hard work.

But perhaps the best way to discover the role of grit in the journey to become known is to examine the life of Brian Meeks. Sometimes grit means that you have to go hungry to achieve your goals.

Brian enjoyed a productive career as a data analyst with a national insurance company when he was lured by an opportunity to go out on his own and lead an independent IT project. He enjoyed the flexibility and independence of his new lifestyle, but after just a year on his own, the contract dried up, and he was out of work.

The beginning of a global financial crisis was a tough time to be looking for a job in Southern California. Companies were announcing massive layoffs, and the expense of living in California rapidly depleted Brian's funds.

To give himself a chance to get back on his feet, he moved from Los Angeles to his grandfather's abandoned home in rural Iowa. The old house was in poor shape after being empty for three years, but at least Brian had a roof over his head, and the house repairs gave him something to occupy his time while he tried to find work.

Brian found that the job market in America's heartland wasn't any better. He cobbled together a few odd jobs and was living on just $500 a month, enough to put food on the table and gas in the car. Then he discovered his sustainable interest ... quite by accident.

"In 2010 I was teaching myself woodworking," he said. "But I learned the hard way that you can't make a table while you're watching a football game. I was so distracted that the table legs all came out different lengths. I thought this was a funny lesson so I posted it on a site I discovered called Blogger. I just wanted to record this funny incident. To my amazement, 300 people saw the post and 25 people left comments asking me to write more.

"Now one thing you must understand: I hated writing with a white-hot passion. My eighth-grade English teacher was so mean that she ruined the subject for me. I went through the rest of my life avoiding writing at all costs. But now I found that people thought I was entertaining ... so I just kept blogging. And I have never missed a day of blogging since that day. The longer I did it, the more confident I became."

On his twenty-ninth day of blogging, Brian wrote the

first chapter of a story idea – the tale of a 1950s-era detective named Henry Wood. His small but growing audience loved it, so he would periodically write another installment in his little mystery manuscript. Nine months later, he had finished an entire novel on his blog. His readers were hooked, so he started another detective novel, and then another. Brian completed three full novels before he had the courage to publish them in book form for all the world to see.

By 2013, he had self-published five books and made a grand total of $5,000 in annual sales. But instead of taking the money and spending it on a vacation or other luxury, he continued to live on $500 a month and used the book revenue to improve the cover art and editing of his next set of books.

The following year Brian published another five books and doubled his annual revenue to $10,000. Once again he plowed all of it back into his publishing venture. Finally, by 2016 he was making more than $10,000 a month from his books, and he finally quit the small job that had been providing his subsistence living.

If you've been keeping score, you've figured out that Brian lived hand-to-mouth and wrote every day for *five years* before he became successful enough to quit his job.

How did he maintain his drive to persist? "Because I could see I was making progress," he said. "Every book did better than the last. People were leaving strong reviews. I was growing more confident in my writing every time I published. I could do the math, and I knew that if I kept at it, stayed disciplined, and kept improving, I could make a decent living ... and more important, have a very flexible lifestyle.

"I think my key to success was that I never set a deadline for myself. As long as things were moving in the right direction, I allowed myself to be patient and keep going. Plus, writing made me happy!"

I interviewed dozens of people for this book, and every single one of them had the grit to persist for years even in the face of significant hurdles. Becoming known is hard work.

When is it time to quit?

Brian Meeks and the other subjects of this book had the mental toughness and discipline to pursue their place and space until they found significant success. But suppose you've followed the path of this book, exhibited vicious consistency and grit, and you're still spinning your wheels.

If you still love what you're doing but see no momentum after at least a year, then perhaps you need an adjustment in one of the four elements I've described in the book:

- **Place:** Maybe your sustainable interest isn't distinctive enough, or you haven't articulated it in a way that people can understand. Revisit the exercises in Chapter 4.

- **Space:** Perhaps you've picked the wrong channel to build your brand, or you underestimated the information density in your niche. Maybe your audience has migrated to another platform since you started (for example, you're blogging and the people who need you are on Snapchat or Instagram).

- **Consistent content:** Perhaps you're not creating enough content to make a difference, or the content is boring. Are you comfortable and having fun with your content, or is it a struggle? Maybe it's time to get some honest feedback on your writing, podcast, or video style.

- **Audience:** Often, people pursue a path and later learn the audience is so small that their dreams simply are not achievable. A pivot would mean expanding the scope of your sustainable interest to include a broader audience.

If one of these scenarios sounds plausible, adjust, pivot, and keep going!

But sometimes the roadblock is insurmountable – perhaps it's even something that's entirely out of your control. No matter how much you plan, sacrifice, and strive, you'll still encounter life in its many forms – illness, a financial crisis, even joyful interruptions like the birth of a child.

The moment you hit a true roadblock is a critical decision point. Is it time to quit?

At these moments, here are a few steps you can take to determine if you should keep pushing or pursue a different path:

1. Look at your measurements of momentum. Are positive things still happening that would indicate better times ahead?

2. Take a break. Yes, consistency is important. But it's also fair to tell your audience that you need some time off. Perhaps the roadblock will sort itself out or you'll gain new insight and energy by establishing a little distance from the work.

3. Talk to others, keeping an open heart and an open mind. There was a point in my life when I had a vision for a new product that I was certain would be a sensation. I worked on this idea for two years but got nowhere. Finally, I talked to a trusted friend who advised me that in the time I had taken to develop this concept, the technology had moved on. I was too late. The feedback hurt, but I was smart enough to know that I couldn't be in love with an idea so much that I denied reality.

4. Assess your grit. Are you built for endurance in the rough times?

Let's unpack this last question a little more. In her seminal book *Grit*,[3] Angela Duckworth describes the four core personality traits of people with the exceptional persistence needed to become known:

- **Love of the work:** Success begins with enjoying what you do. Every gritty person Angela studied for her book can point to aspects of their work they enjoy less than others, and most have to put up with chores they don't enjoy at all. Nevertheless, they're captivated by the endeavor as a whole. With enduring fascination and childlike curiosity, they practically shout, "I love what I do!"

- **Capacity to practice:** Nobody is born an expert, so after defining your sustainable interest, you must devote yourself to the focused, full-hearted, challenge-exceeding practice that leads to mastery. You must zero in on your weaknesses and commit to improve, week after month after year. To be gritty is to resist complacency. "Whatever it takes, I want to improve!" is a refrain of all paragons of grit, no matter their particular interest or how excellent they already are.

- **Purpose:** For most people, an interest without purpose is nearly impossible to sustain for a lifetime. Gritty people are driven because they can say, "My work is important – both to me and to others."

- **Hope:** Hope is a rising-to-the-occasion kind of perseverance. From the very beginning to the very end, it's important to keep going even when things are difficult, even when you have doubts. At various points, in big ways and small, you get knocked down. If you stay down, grit loses. If you get up, grit prevails.

When people drop out, it's probably due to some deficit in one of these characteristics. If you find any of these thoughts going through your head you're probably at the end of the trail:

- "I'm bored."

- "The effort isn't worth it."

- "This isn't important to me."

- "I can't do this, so I might as well give up."

There's nothing wrong with having thoughts like these. But if one of these statements is the story in your head right now, it's time to do a U-turn and try another path.

An insurmountable roadblock is not the same as a downfall. It's a chance to take control. Honestly addressing the issues in an ego-free manner will help you avoid years of frustration and move you on a more fruitful journey. A roadblock is a reminder that we have more growing to do and new parts of ourselves to discover.

Our time together is almost through. We have one more chapter to go. Let's hear some final words of advice from those gritty people who have become known ... and I still have a surprise or two in store for you.

CHAPTER 11

The Care and Nurturing of KNOWN

"Just keep swimming." – Dory the fish

It's time to wind things down (sniff).

Are you fired up? Are you ready to become known? OK! This chapter is meant to give you a final dose of inspiration to accompany you through the exciting journey ahead.

The case for consistency

This word.

Consistency.

It's been used so many times in this book that I considered making it the fifth step in the process. But the truth is, consistency isn't a "step," it's the bedrock for it all.

Certainly, no amount of planning, prepping, hoping, wishing, or dreaming will make any difference in your potential to become known if you don't show up on a regular basis. Consistent effort propels you to be known, and it keeps you there.

You know, it's been a long book, and if you've beat the odds to make it this far, you deserve a reward. Here's a bit of relevant poetry from our next guest star:

> *Go the distance.*
> *Do it with grace or do it ugly,*
> *because some days*
> *that's what your best looks like.*
> *It only matters*
> *that you go the full heart distance.*

This bit of loveliness comes from Anna Blake, an author and poet who established herself as the Bard of the American Prairie and a leading voice of horse advocacy. Anna's effort to become known has been as steady as the warm summer rain. She's blogged at least twice a week without fail for seven years.

Anna's dream was to write a book, but she was overwhelmed by the thought of it. After all, her home is a place called Infinity Farm, a ranch poking out of the treeless Colorado prairie. For most of her life, the only "audience" Anna has ever known has been her grasslands herd of horses, llamas, goats, ducks, dogs, cats, and her heart and soul, a mule named Edgar Rice Burro. Not exactly the inner circle of literary culture.

But Anna also knew that she had access to a digital world where anything is possible, no matter who you are or where you live, as long as you have an internet connection, a keyboard, and a strong will.

"I've always known I had a book in me," she said, "but I was paralyzed by the idea of starting. I had a lot to say, but didn't have confidence that I could do it, and I didn't have an audience who would read it. So I started small.

"I began a blog about my love of the ranch and, in particular, my horses. To force myself to become a better writer, I gave myself writing assignments – write something poignant, describe something hard to describe, be funny. I was consciously tuning up my skills.

"How I wrote was as important as what I wrote; my standard was to do my best every time. The hardest part, always, was to hit that publish button. I was still confidence-free. Who did I think I was, after all? For the first couple of years, a grand total of 11 friends read my posts."

But she stuck with it. Today, Anna is among the most well-known and beloved equine authors in the world. She's published three books, her blog has attracted more than a million page views, and she's a recipient of the prestigious Reader's Choice Award for animal-related works of nonfiction.

Consistency heals a multitude of faults

"Consistency is about the only thing that's within my control," she said. "I don't have a college degree, I don't have important friends, and I'm not much of a joiner. The biggest thing I have going for me is that I can choose to push on through. I believe in that quote about persistence being more important than talent.

"I set time aside to write every day and I give myself deadlines. It's a simple plan, but simple and easy aren't the same thing. In time, my writing improved, readers were kind, and things got easier.

"Consistency can heal a multitude of faults ... and maybe it eventually turns into talent. It's discipline, I guess, but I literally push distracting thoughts out of my mind. I guard my creativity and dismiss negative chatter. Ignoring doubts is serious weight-lifting, but before long it becomes a habit. Then the more you push through, the stronger you feel. Maybe it's consistency that makes me steadfast, or maybe vice versa. What matters is creating a circle of thought that says yes instead of no."

How much is enough?

Like Anna Blake, every successful person in this book achieved their goals by defining a place, establishing a space, and creating content with regularity. So what does "regularity" mean? How much is enough?

There's no standard answer, of course. Artist Lorraine Loots and author Brian Meeks have posted their content every single day for years. Marketoonist Tom Fishburne publishes a cartoon in a newsletter once a week. Avinash Kaushik of Google creates his mega-blog posts just once a month or so.

Unfortunately, there's no secret formula for figuring out how frequently you need to post your content. The most important thing is to find a schedule that works for you. If you're starting out in most fields, one piece of rich content a week is a reasonable goal.

Mitch Joel is a pioneering blogger who has published three to four times a week for more than a decade. He's written two books and hosts two weekly podcasts. For Mitch, creating content has become an essential part of his life.

"To a lot of people, producing content might seem like a drug – you do it to be successful, you need to keep feeding the beast," he said. "But it doesn't have to be a beast. If you love what you do and you spend your time engrossed in it because you're passionate and persistent, I don't think there's any problem blogging with regularity. I find it hard to decide what to blog about. I almost have too much to chat about and share.

"For the best content creators out there, it's not a burden. It's totally in the flow of their values and who they are."

People who become known commit to a schedule and stick to it because there are so many benefits to creating a content rhythm:

- Being consistent forces you to always have the creative juices flowing. You're in a continuous process of brainstorming ideas that will delight your audience. Even if no one is reading or viewing your content (and you can expect this at first!), creating content stretches you creatively.

- Consistency creates committed readers. By posting reliably, your audience comes to know when they should drop in to find something new. In a way, it takes the pressure off of blasting social channels or drawing everyone in again each time you have something new to say.

- Creating content regularly helps you find your voice and develop your style. Often, a sustainable interest only takes root and blooms based on feedback from your audience over time. No content, no audience ... no feedback.

- The more regularly you publish, the more quickly you'll build up your site with content that can be discovered and shared.

There's no better time to pull the cord and get going. A year from now you could have hundreds of posts in your archives, or you could keep putting it off and have zero.

What seems like a chore at first can become the fabric of your life. An experiment rolls into a rhythm. The rhythm drives momentum. Momentum turns into the thunderclap of a new movement. Insecurity eventually gets drowned out by the applause of new fans.

So it's time to start, commit ... and believe.

Constancy and challenge

In this book, I've tried to encourage and inspire, but also tackle the hard questions with unvarnished and compassionate advice. I want to shine a strong, clear light on both the good and the ugly, and if something on the path is hard to do, I've been honest about that.

Chris Brogan knows the hard path to becoming known. He's risen to the top of his field of entrepreneurial thought leadership through tireless work and unlimited generosity of time and spirit. He's built his personal brand by creating some form of content every day of his life for more than 15 years. And he's done it while battling depression.

Chris has contributed an essay for this book, explaining how to stay on a path toward becoming known even when the chemicals in your head are telling you "no:"

> It's weird being known for being an entrepreneur and author who openly talks about his depression. I'm grateful in many ways, because it also means that others might see what I'm doing and talking about and take something from it for themselves. It's with that in mind that I want to talk about my success and how depression played a role.

> You'd be wrong to say "Chris is successful DESPITE his depression." The thing with any mental illness (man, that makes it sound really huge but I only have "mild clinical depression") is that it's part of you. Everyone just has different cards to play, different abilities. My son is a highly functioning autistic who is incredible with music, software, and all kinds of creative pursuits. He's very social, very passionate, and also still needs help getting his socks on sometimes. I don't know that he wants to be autistic, but I know it's not a hindrance in any large way to him.

I'm successful and I happen to deal with depression.

My take on content is that it's the campfire we gather around. Quick. Without thinking. Who's your favorite Star Wars character? Mine's Boba Fett. But you and I couldn't talk about that if we didn't have the "content" of Star Wars already.

It's your job to make that fire (your content) worth gathering around.

Depression doesn't care if you have deadlines. When I'm hit with it, I really just want to stay in bed. I might read, watch YouTube, scroll to the bottom of Facebook. Oh wait. There's no bottom? Okay, then!

Instead, I think this really simple thought: Let me go be helpful for a minute. That's all it takes to get me to write a piece for a blog post or a course or whatever book I'm writing. On the day I'm writing these words to you, I can feel depression tugging at my sleeve. It wants my attention, but I've been ignoring it quite a lot. Because I have work to do. I wanted to write this so you'd see what depression is all about. You can deal with depression AND create content.

Content yields connections. That's the goal. One way that people connect with me is that they know I'm that guy who writes about depression sometimes. They ask me how to get out of bed. They ask me what gets me back on my feet. They ask me if they can still succeed. (Yes!)

Find your own way to the success you want. Make your own game and then win at it.

If you need help with your depression, get it. If you need meds, take them. If you have days where sleep is all you can do, sleep. And then find your way out to create something when you get a moment. Doesn't have to be big. Sometimes, I just go on Instagram and post a picture of me waving to the camera. If nothing else, it shows that I'm here and that depression is a jerk, but he's my jerk. Do what you can. It's all good.

And if ever you want to say, "Hey, I deal with depression, too," then I'm eager to hear from you. My doors are always open.

Final thoughts from the stars

The theory behind this book coalesced through discussions with more than 100 amazing people, many of whom you've met in the preceding chapters. I asked a few of them to provide some final words of encouragement. If they could say one thing to embolden you, my readers, to start on the path to become known, what would they tell you?

> "Nothing replaces perseverance. Lots of people have talent, and few convert that talent into something meaningful. Decide to do something, and persevere. If a project fails, don't let it be from not having tried hard enough and kept going long enough. Some projects will fail, and you have to move on to something else. But there's nothing sadder than seeing a project die before its time." – **Dr. Jamie Goode, wine blogger**

> "Remember that everybody starts at the bottom. When I started making my videos, my mom had to help me financially for some time. I had to be resilient and keep working on great content for my audience. I believed in what I was doing but it took three years for things to fall into place. It finally happened like magic and now I have enough spon-

sors to make a living. Don't be afraid to start small and learn, learn, learn along the way." **– Isadora Becker, Brazilian YouTube foodie**

"It may sound like a cliché, but don't be afraid to put your work out there. So many hide away, waiting for the 'perfect' moment in their work, and so they're never seen. The great thing about the format of my project was that I had to post paintings every single day, even before I was happy with them or felt they were complete. What's amazing is that not only did it force me to take myself less seriously, but it also helped me realize that this is how some of my most popular art was made! Do good work – a lot of it – and put it out there consistently. I really do believe that's the core of it." **– Lorraine Loots, world-famous painter of miniature art**

"With all the opportunities for self-publishing, you don't have to be Deepak Chopra to write something. Everybody is, or can be, an expert on something. Take me. I haven't been in the kitchen in 20 years. I hate eating vegan. But how hard would it be to read every book on veganism, buy some ingredients, and then write a little book: The Non-Vegan's Vegan Cookbook?" **– James Altucher, failed-investor-turned-self-help-guru**

"Provide value with the expectation that you'll never receive anything in return. Serve your audience with your arms wide open, not with a hand extended." **– Shawn Van Dyke, construction industry consultant**

"Resilience is an imperative. I believe in resilience so much and if I had to pick just one character trait for success it would be that. I recognize there are certain situations when it's no longer smart to persevere. Sometimes it's best to start over and rethink things. You have to know when to make the pivot. But too many people quit too soon." – **Zander Zon, YouTube bassist**

"My number one piece of advice is to be selfless and empower others. Maybe it's my Christian upbringing, but giving of myself with no thought of return is part of my makeup. Whatever your belief system, if you give selflessly of your own skills, expertise, and passion, then God/Karma/the Universe will look after you and repay you for your contribution to the sum of human experience." – **Pete Matthew, financial planner**

"Making some impact on the world might seem like an overwhelming proposition. Maybe you want to do something big, but you have limited resources. There is time for everything. Taking baby steps is perfectly fine. My biggest piece of advice is to simply do it, get like-minded people on your side and really go for it. There are always surprises and opportunities around every corner. Have fun and enjoy what you've created. Never lose sight of why you started your own movement and keep going even when you're unsure of your impact." – **Jennifer James, founder of Social Good Moms**

"Love what you do. I know everyone says that, but deeply and truly, love the details. Nothing is more attractive than seeing passion in action. Be wildly honest, especially about your weaknesses; it ends up being a huge relief. Finally, make it a rule to say 'yes' and 'thank you' every chance you get, because it leaves a good taste in your mouth." – **Anna Blake, writer**

227

And one more

Over the last few years I've been supporting the efforts of an extraordinary woman named Diana Krahn. She has dedicated her life to helping people in crisis, most notably rescuing women and children who have been captured in the path of ISIS and then hidden away in the underground world of sex slavery.

Through her work Diana has put herself in harm's away and looked terror in the face. She is among the bravest individuals I've ever known. But she didn't start that way. In fact, Diana comes from the world of public relations and advertising. She was a high-powered fashion industry executive based in Paris, networking between media appearances and the glamour of Cannes and the Riviera.

How and why did she make such a profound change? How did she find the courage to drop everything, start something so dramatically new, and keep it up for years in the face of danger and even death?

I'll let Diana tell you, in her own words:

> For much of my life I was convicted to help others. As a child I worked side by side with Mother Teresa in the slums of Calcutta. My parents worked selflessly for the poor, beginning each day with a question: "What can we do to help others today?" My family founded an orphanage that has nurtured more than a hundred children in India.
>
> Serving others was literally seared into my soul. But as an adult, I was afraid to do anything about it. The problems of our world seemed so big, and I was so incredibly small. What could I possibly do to create any kind of meaningful change in the world? And then I remembered an event from when I was a child …

My aunt worked with Mother Teresa for many years. I would visit my aunt in the slums of Calcutta and I would work right alongside her. When I met Mother Teresa for the first time, I was just 8 years old. So I didn't see her in the way that adults would, I guess. I saw her as this very caring, wonderful, elderly lady who just genuinely loved the poor.

Perhaps she was the most authentic person I've ever met. She wasn't simply a saint in front of the TV cameras or when speaking before the United Nations. She was precisely the same person everywhere ... behind closed doors, to the poorest of the poor, and to me. That was the most touching and inspiring thing to witness.

Of course the shock of stepping from a life of privilege into abject poverty when I visited Mother Teresa was a dizzying sensation. I was a little girl! What could I do to help? There were so many people who needed so much! I was overcome by the immensity of the poverty, the grime, and suffering. What difference could I possibly make?

Mother Teresa sensed my internal struggle. I suppose my reaction was probably quite common to almost everyone who entered her world for the first time.

She took me aside, bent down and said to me in her gentle voice, "Diana, you seem so overwhelmed. And you seem so fascinated by how it all works and you want to help. But you see, I started very small. Everything good and great starts as something small.

Whatever change happens in the world normally begins with little acts. Start with the small kindness. Just care for people. Love people. Stop judging others. When you judge people, you don't have time to love them. So it doesn't matter who they are, or where they're from, or what they look like, just reach out to them. Maybe one act of kindness seems unimportant when there's so much suffering. Maybe you feel like one raindrop in an ocean of need. But even the ocean is not complete without that single raindrop. Just care. Just love. Just take one step. The raindrop matters."

That was something I could do, even when I was 8. And that's something that we all can do. Not everybody is in a position to do great things, but all of us can accomplish small things. We can all reach out to one person in need, create one act of kindness, take one step forward, begin something new.

A beautiful story, from a beautiful person. Sometimes, I've felt like that raindrop too. I've wondered if all this work makes a difference. But then, every once in a while, I get a glimpse of the ocean.

Last year I was the keynote speaker at a conference in Scotland, and a young woman came up to me and extended her hand. I had never met her before ... in fact, I didn't recognize her name, Chloe Forbes-Kindlen.

"I have wanted to meet you for so long," she said excitedly. "I've read your blog for years, and all of your books. You were one of the few people who took the time to answer my questions online when I asked you something. You gave me the confidence to start my blog and a new business. I do what I do today because of you. I am who I am today because of you."

There were tears welling in Chloe's eyes. And mine, too.

I said to her, "The thing about it is, I am who I am because of you, too."

When I started my own journey to become known, nobody read my blog. I had no idea what I was doing. My first posts were awful, and my confidence was fragile. But I was determined and consistent. I became better, bolder, and more self-assured as the years flew by.

I wrote when I was exhausted. I wrote when I was so sick I couldn't get out of bed. I published at least twice a week, every week, for eight years.

And at that moment with Chloe, tears running down both of our faces, I knew every bit of that struggle was worthwhile.

I'm so thankful I took that step. I'm so proud that I kept at it, through everything. My blog posts were a raindrop in the endless ocean of content. But that ocean is not complete without me.

And you.

It's your turn to be known.

Keep learning about *KNOWN*

Please visit our website www.known-book.com to learn about:

- Updates and new case studies

- Exclusive training and coaching programs associated with *KNOWN*

- Special offers for educators

- Bulk book sales

There is a helpful workbook that accompanies this book available on Amazon. Find additional exercises and bonus material in *The KNOWN Personal Branding Workbook.*

References

Chapter One

1. "How to become famous in three easy steps" by Drew Kimble http://skinnyartist.com/how-to-become-famous-in-3-easy-steps/

2. Most of this story was generated through a personal interview I conducted with Antonio Centeno. A few details were filled in from an interview between Antonio and David Garland. https://therisetothetop.com/interviews-guests/antonio-centeno-200-videos-200-days/

3. The facts from this case study on Joe Wicks comes from an article published in the London *Guardian* in 2015: https://www.theguardian.com/lifeandstyle/2016/jun/18/joe-wicks-meet-body-coach-million-dollar-muscles

4. This quote came the the London *Guardian* "Supertrainer Joe Wicks on Instagram Pelifies and his fitness philosophy" "http://www.standard.co.uk/lifestyle/health/supertrainer-joe-wicks-on-instagram-pelfies-and-his-fitness-philosophy-a3258186.html

5. Excerpt From: Angela Duckworth. *"Grit."* iBooks. https://itun.es/us/O8fC8.l

Chapter Two

1. This Gary Vaynerchuk quote came from his Udemy course on personal branding.

2. Altucher, James "What I learned about life after interviewing 80 highly successful people" http://www.jamesaltucher.com/2015/01/what-i-learned-about-life-after-interviewing-80-highly-successful-people/

3. These quotes from Tom Webster first appeared on The Marketing Companion podcast in August, 2016. In the original dialogue Tom attributed the idea of "top-of-mind preference" to our friend Tom Martin.

Chapter Three

1. Clark, Dorie (2015-04-21). *Stand Out: How to Find Your Breakthrough Idea and Build a Following Around It* (p. 37). Penguin Publishing Group. Kindle Edition.

Chapter Five

1. Some of the stories and quotes in the James Altucher section came from a profile about him that appeared in *The New York Times*: http://www.nytimes.com/2016/08/07/fashion/james-altucher-self-help-guru.html

Chapter Seven

1. Quote from Elsie Larson comes from A Beautiful Mess

website: http://www.abeautifulmess.com/

Chapter Ten

1. Ira Glass quote from the book *Roadmap* by Roadtrip Nation, copyright 2015, Chronicle Books

2. Buzzfeed "13 Charts That Will Make Total Sense to People With Impostor Syndrome." https://www.buzzfeed.com/kristinchirico/13-charts-that-will-make-total-sense-to-people-with-impostor

3. Excerpt From: Angela Duckworth. *"Grit."* iBooks. https://itun.es/us/O8fC8.l

The Stars of *KNOWN*

Continue to follow your favorite stars from *KNOWN* by discovering them on the web (in order of appearance):

Chapter 1
Larry C. Lewis works in the jewelry industry and is stepping out on his own at marketinglikeapro.net.

Antonio Centeno – You can find out more about Antonio and his fashion videos at www.realmenrealstyle.com.

Joe Wicks is now a famous personal trainer. You can find him at www.thebodycoach.com.

Lorraine Loots continues to display her extraordinary miniature paintings at www.lorraineloots.com.

Angela Duckworth is a MacArthur "genius" grant winner, researcher, and author of *Grit: The Power of Passion and Perseverance*. You can follow her at www.angeladuckworth.com.

Lindsey Kirchoff has moved on from her "How to Market to Me" days and you can keep up with her at www.lindseykirchoff.com.

Chapter 2

Gary Vaynerchuk spreads the gospel of hustle at www.gary-vaynerchuk.com.

James Altucher pens his unorthodox view of the world at www.jamesaltucher.com.

Tom Webster is a vice president at Edison Research. He co-hosts a podcast with Mark Schaefer called The Marketing Companion and he blogs at www.brandsavant.com.

Betty Brennan, the world's greatest physical storyteller, leads her team at www.taylorstudios.com.

Chapter 3

Ann Handley is the author of *Everybody Writes*. You can learn more about Ann at www.annhandey.com.

Jon Briggs delivers his irreverent anti-fan products at www.parodytease.com.

Fanny Slater – You can get your fanny in the kitchen at www.fannyslater.com.

Jane Hart is an expert in workplace learning. You can follow her at www.janehart.com.

Sally Hogshead is the author of *Fascinate* and can be found at www.howtofascinate.com.

Drew Houston is the founder of Dropbox.

Martin Lindstrom wrote Small Data and can be found at www.martinlindstrom.com.

Peter Thiel is the co-founder of Paypal.

Dorie Clark is a consultant and author of Stand Out. You can find her at www.dorieclark.com.

Chapter 4

Jamie Goode – The pioneering wine blogger can be found www.wineanorak.com.

Greg Kinman, the retired teacher, shoots his guns on his YouTube channel https://www.youtube.com/user/hickok45

Chapter 5

Isadora Becker provides her cooking videos at https://www.youtube.com/user/gastronomismo.

Suzy Trotta's real estate agency is www.trottamontgomery.com and you can also find her fun pictures on Instagram.

Rand Fishkin provides his Whiteboard Friday videos at www.moz.com.

Tom Fishburne delivers his hilarious cartoons at www.marketoonist.com

John Lee Dumas hosts his well-known podcast at www.eofire.com.

Avinash Kaushik of Google publishes his epic blog posts at www.kaushik.net.

JuanPa Zurita can be found on YouTube https://www.youtube.

com/channel/UCUo7T81zvCqpPhfsPb_kajA

Shawn Van Dyke is growing his construction consulting business at www.shawnvandyke.com/

Christopher Korody publishes his drone site at www.drone-businesscenter.com.

Scott Monty creates his digital marketing newsletter at www.scottmonty.com.

Chapter 6
Jeff Bullas blogs at www.jeffbullas.com.

Jenni Prokopy provides her health and relationship advice at www.chronicbabe.com.

Mimi Thorisson creates her stunning Manger blog at www.MimiThorisson.com.

Ben Wellington offers his entertaining statistical insights at www.IQuantNY.com.

Glennon Doyle Melton issues her award-winning advice on www.momastery.com.

Chapter 7
Elsie Larson is one of the sisters behind the DIY megasite www.abeautifulmess.com.

Mike Masse has a massive following for his acoustic music covers at https://www.youtube.com/user/mikemassedotcom.

Alice Ackerman is on the staff of Virginia Tech University

http://medicine.vtc.vt.edu/people/alice-d-ackerman/.

Chad Pollitt is a founder of Relevance Agency and creates content at www.relevance.com.

Sarah Mason helped create the design of this book and can be found at http://uncommonlysocial.com/.

Ana Silva O'Reilly has her luxury travel blog at www.mrsoaroundtheworld.com.

Ian Cleary, the master networker, is an entrepreneur at www.razorsocial.com.

Aaron Lee, the Malaysian fashion phenom has his site at www.askaaronlee.com.

Chapter 8

Lee Odden is a marketing thought leader who blogs at www.toprankingmarketing.com.

Tamsen Webster helps people create amazing speeches at www.tamsenwebster.com.

Chapter 9

Pete Matthew, an unconventional financial planner, produces content at www.meaningfulmoney.tv.

Zander Zon, an extraordinary bassist posts his music videos at https://www.youtube.com/user/Zander4724.

Neale Godfrey, the banker-turned-author has her online home at Amazon where you can see her books: www.amazon.com/

Neale-S.-Godfrey/e/B00lIO9KNU

Felix Kjellberg (aka PewDiePie) is hard to miss on YouTube: https://www.youtube.com/user/PewDiePie.

Jennifer James, a mom blogger changing the world, can be found at https://mombloggersforsocialgood.com/.

Chapter 10
Paul Roetzer, a man who decided to NOT be known founded www.pr2020.com.

Ira Glass, host of This American Life, is online here: https://www.thisamericanlife.org/contributors/ira-glass.

John Espirian, a technical writer beginning his journey to become known, posts at http://espirian.co.uk/.

Brian Meeks sacrificed for five years to become known. You can read more about him at http://extremelyaverage.com/.

Chapter 11
Anna Blake, the bard of the prairie, is online at https://anna-blake.com.

Mitch Joel is a leader of the global Mirum Agency. His blog and podcast can be found at www.mitchjoel.com.

Chris Brogan advises his readers on entrepreneurship at www.chrisbrogan.com.

Diana Krahn is fighting for the rights of oppressed women and children at www.dianajkrahn.com

Chloe Forbes-Kindlen creates content and tutorials at http://
c4compete.com/

Determining content density in regions of the world

Chapter 4 set out a simple method of determining the on-line competition for your sustainable interest by conducting a Google search. If you want a more refined search, or if you need to narrow this down to the opportunity in a certain country, you'll have to follow a few additional steps.

This is a process called the Keyword Optimization Index (KOI) contributed to this book by Roy Ishak, an award-winning copywriter and SEO specialist from The Netherlands:

- Step 1: Use the Keyword Planner of Google AdWords or another keyword suggestion tool to determine the search volume of your focus keywords.

- Step 2: Find out how much competition you have by Googling: *allintitle:keyword* (the keyword would be something related to your sustainable interest).

- Step 3: Divide the search volume (the size of your market

from the Keyword Planner) by the amount of "allintitle" search results (your competition) and multiply that number by the search volume again. For example:

Search volume: *100,000 results*

Search results (competition): *2,000,000 results*

Formula: *100,000 / 2,000,000 x 100,000 = 5,000*

Do this test for a variety of keywords to determine which ones are the most popular and have the least competition – regardless of the population of a country. The higher the resulting number, the higher your chance to rank well in the organic search results of Google and the higher your chance of succeeding in this market.

If you're trying to dominate a niche in a specific region of the world, narrow your investigation by country:

To adjust **search volume,** every keyword suggestion tool has an option to "select country." For example, if you select "The Netherlands," the tool shows you only the search volumes of Holland.

For the **competition factor,** every person around the globe uses their own national version of Google. People in America use google.com. Citizens in the Netherlands would use google.nl, in France it would be google.fr, etc. When you use *"allintitle:keyword"* filter in the version of Google for a certain country, Google displays the competition you would be facing for results in that country.

Acknowledgments

Can you imagine getting an email from a complete stranger asking if he can interview you for a book? I am so grateful to the dozens of astonishing people who somehow trusted me enough to answer the call and tell their story of *KNOWN*. This project was a team effort and could not have been accomplished without the amazing stories of people who worked for years to become known. THANK YOU to you all!

In Appendix I, I've listed some details about the stars of *KNOWN* but there are many others who have helped me make these connections behind the scenes like Mitch Joel, Gregory Pouy, Lauren Schaefer, Jeffery Slater, Kerry O'Shea Gorgone, Chris Marr, Tony Dowling, and C.C. Chapman.

Mandy Edwards provided editorial support throughout this process and helped me come up with the research and facts to make the stories of *KNOWN* complete, accurate, and entertaining. Bernadette Jiwa has been my cherished sounding board for years now and her light and accurate creative touch is a blessing.

When my brain hurts, I ask Christopher S. Penn for help. Chris has helped me untangle vexing book-related problems for years! Thank you, sir.

My friend Kitty Kilian read every word of my manuscript and took special care in challenging my assumptions. Kitty helped me write with a truly global perspective. Her wisdom and honest feedback made this book so much better!

I have a trusted group of friends who offered to poke holes in my manuscript along the way including Danielle Rogers, Professor Denny McCorkle, Rhonda Hurwitz, Andrew M. Smith, Matt Hannaford, Alisa Meredith, Natchi Lazarus, Ana Silva O'Reilly, Jennifer Porter, and Kiki Schirr. I am especially indebted to Jayme Soulati, Valentina Escobar-Gonzalez, and Corina Manea for their careful examination of each phrase and idea!

My "dream team" who helped me create such a beautiful book include my editor Elizabeth Rea and art designer Sarah Mason.

Many thanks to Joe and Kathleen Atkins for their photographic support for my books over many years.

Last but not least, I owe so much to my wife Rebecca whose patient encouragement and wise counsel soothed me throughout the gut-wrenching process of writing this book.

All my gifts come from God. My prayer is that this book has glorified Him in some small way.

About the Author

Mark W. Schaefer is a globally-recognized speaker, educator, business consultant, and author who blogs at {grow} — one of the top marketing blogs of the world.

Mark has worked in global sales, PR, and marketing positions for more than 30 years and now provides consulting services as Executive Director of U.S.-based Schaefer Marketing Solutions. He specializes in strategy development, personal branding, and digital marketing training and clients include both start-ups and global brands such as Dell, Johnson & Johnson, Adidas, and the U.S. Air Force.

Mark has advanced degrees in marketing and organizational development and is a faculty member of the graduate studies program at Rutgers University. A career highlight was studying under Peter Drucker while studying for his MBA.

He is the author of five other best-selling books, *Social Media Explained, Return On Influence, Born to Blog, The Content Code, and The Tao of Twitter,* the best-selling book on Twitter in the world. Please join him on The Marketing Companion podcast, which he co-hosts with Tom Webster.

He is among the world's most recognized social media authorities and has been a keynote speaker at many conferences around the world including Social Media Week London, National Economic Development Association, the Institute for International and European Affairs, and Word of Mouth Marketing Summit Tokyo.

You can stay connected with Mark at www.Businesses-GROW.com and by following his adventures and stories on Twitter: @markwschaefer

INDEX